Everyone agrees with TOM!

Everyone agrees with TOM!

Who appreciates and/or uses TOM principles?

Some without even realising it? And perhaps the more consciously we use the TOM principles, the better the results.

Gordon Bethune, CEO Continental Airlines 1994-2004 – Author of 'From Worst to First' with Scott Huler:
'Tell them what you want, reward them for it, and get out of the way.'
… or in TOM language:
'Tell them what you want = set meaningful **Objectives**
…reward them for it = add a **Motivational** *factor*
…and get out of the way = **Trust** them to do their job

Jack Welch, Chairman and CEO of General Electric, 1981-2001:
'If you pick the right people and give them the opportunity to spread their wings (**Trust** them) *and put compensation as a carrier behind it* (**Motivation**) *you almost don't have to manage them.'* (set their **Objectives**).

Sir Richard Branson, Virgin Group Chairman, Author of 'Richard Branson – the autobiography'
'I have no secret. There are no rules to follow in business. I just work hard (set and achieve **Objectives**) *and, as I always have done, believe I can do it* (**Trust** myself). *Most of all, though, I try to have fun.'* (**Motivating** factor)

Paul Hopwood, Mindshop (International business advisory and facilitation services)
'I have read your book! There are many things that align with my thinking. … I really enjoyed your take on the concept.'

Heidi Palmer, TNT - ICS Express
'TOM is really making a difference to how our managers communicate and manage their teams. The models are simple and just make sense'.

Everyone agrees with

TOM!

...and they want some of what TOM has...
Happiness, Success, Great Relationships

'TOM shows us
how to achieve
everything we
set out to do.'

ROSS PAGE

Everyone agrees with TOM!

Also Available by this author:

THE ENLIGHTENED RESPONSE

Order this book online at www.trafford.com/07-0601
or email orders@trafford.com

Most Trafford titles are also available at major online book retailers.

Note for Librarians: A cataloguing record for this book is available from Library
and Archives Canada at www.collectionscanada.ca/amicus/index-e.html

Printed in Victoria, BC, Canada.

Designed and typeset in Palatino Linotype, Eras Demi ITC, Gill Sans Ultra Bold.

ISBN: 978-1-4251-2199-0

*We at Trafford believe that it is the responsibility of us all, as both individuals
and corporations, to make choices that are environmentally and socially sound.
You, in turn, are supporting this responsible conduct each time you purchase a
Trafford book, or make use of our publishing services. To find out how you are
helping, please visit www.trafford.com/responsiblepublishing.html*

*Our mission is to efficiently provide the world's finest, most comprehensive
book publishing service, enabling every author to experience success.
To find out how to publish your book, your way, and have it available
worldwide, visit us online at www.trafford.com/10510*

 www.trafford.com

North America & international
toll-free: 1 888 232 4444 (USA & Canada)
phone: 250 383 6864 ♦ fax: 250 383 6804 ♦ email: info@trafford.com

The United Kingdom & Europe
phone: +44 (0)1865 722 113 ♦ local rate: 0845 230 9601
facsimile: +44 (0)1865 722 868 ♦ email: info.uk@trafford.com

10 9 8 7 6 5 4

Dedication and Acknowledgements

I dedicate this book to Diane; my beautiful and patient wife, constant companion and playmate who has allowed TOM to share our life for almost five years.
Also sharing our journey have been our four wonderful children – Mike, Christiaan, Stacey and Emily – who love us, teach us and support us and are a constant source of inspiration and joy.

In addition, I would like to thank my family, friends, colleagues, contacts, trainees, students, clients, acquaintances, books, movies, courses, teachers, schools, television shows, plays… I can't think of a single person, situation or event that hasn't taught me something about how to not only survive, but succeed in this messy and complicated tale I call my life. As corny as it may sound, I do honestly attempt to see the learning in every moment of time, every person and every event – and this of course has had a major influence on the creation of the TOM concepts. As Richard Bach wrote in his book *Illusions*:
'In life, you are either learning something or having fun'.
Most of the time for me it seems to be both, simultaneously.

Thank you all for being an integral part of my and TOM's life.

Specifically to do with getting TOM out of my mind and into print, I would like to thank for their time and support:
Anthony Tindale, Pete Brown, John and Bev Page, Terry Page and Margaret Wyatt, Lynn Hitchcock, Nicky Warham, Steve Rhodes, Heidi Palmer, Ian McGarry, Alistair Bell, Rita Brummer, David Edwards, Arcadia Love, Susan Young, Will Moore, Colin Gaffney, Paul Hopwood… and anyone else who has offered a personal perspective on TOM. I'm sorry if your name is missing from this list - your omission is definitely not intentional.

Everyone agrees with TOM!

Contents

Everyone agrees with TOM!

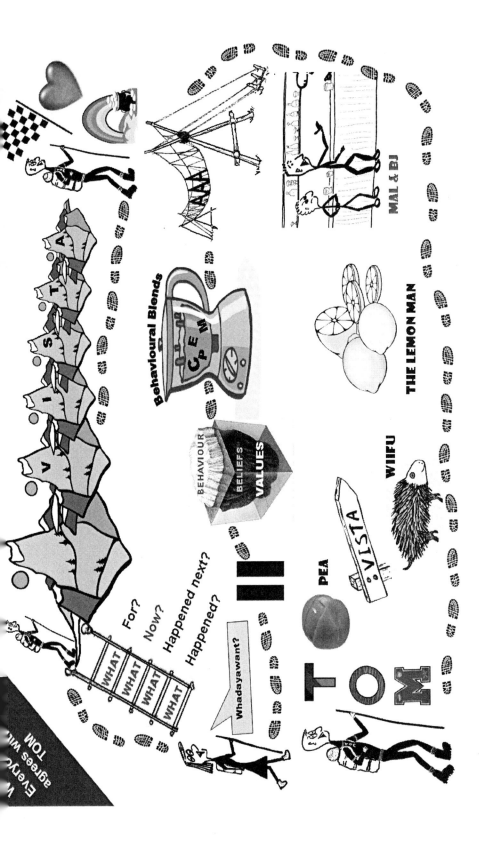

Everyone agrees with TOM!

Introduction ...and yes, I know it looks like a kids' book!

Why does everyone agree with TOM?

TOM has a way of communicating with people that makes them want to agree with him. Whatever it is he is talking about, they feel like they want to help him with it.  Why do they feel that way? This book will explain the basic principles of 'how to get people, including yourself, to get things done and still have a good time'. Or in the business world it's called something like... improve *productivity and satisfaction* levels. When you get right down to it, isn't that what we mean when we say we're having a good life – we're getting things done and having a good time? What if the meaning of 'having a good life' is as simple as getting the balance right between *Tasks and Feelings*?

We share this planet with around six and a half billion human beings – not to mention the billions and billions of other creatures. As much as we would like to think that we are strong and independent individuals, the truth is, we simply could not survive happily and successfully without an ability to communicate with and influence other living things – human, animal or vegetable.

Everyone agrees with TOM!

This book is about achieving results and enjoying the journey. It could also be invaluable to anyone who wants to get on better with others, or conversely, anyone who sometimes clashes with others and wants to figure out how to change that.

For such a huge topic, why is it such a small book? ...because it really is very simple. And yes, yes, I know... it looks like a kids' book! You know why? Because kids don't make a huge fuss over learning like us adults do. This book has been structured using the very latest in En-Lightning Learning techniques – techniques that not only make learning lightning fast, illuminating and effective, but also more enjoyable and easy for the human mind to absorb and act on.

The human brain has many different types of intelligence. Dr Howard Gardner identified eight different methods the brain uses for storing information. And in the mid nineteen-eighties something called Emotional Intelligence emerged, which can either be seen as something separate, or something that's triggered by the initial eight. The theory suggests that, in the long run, how we feel is far more important to us than what we think or do. And to these nine we will add Drama Intelligence – the part of us that links thoughts with stories and dramatic, exciting or scary events.

Note: As part of the 'story' of you reading this book, you may need to return to certain sections to remind yourself of what some terms or phrases mean. At these points you may become irritated that you need reminding, but please remember to accept that this is indeed an integral phase of the learning and remembering process. The act of reviewing the information will reinforce what you have learned by adding yet another string of neurons to your vast and incredibly complex neuro-net.

So now we use all these intelligences to create En-Lightning Learning and the list looks like this:

Musical intelligence (music/rhythm smart)
Intrapersonal intelligence (self smart)
Logical intelligence (logic/reasoning smart)
Drama intelligence (story smart)

Kinesthetic intelligence (sense smart)
Emotional intelligence (feeling smart)
Linguistic intelligence (word smart)
Visual intelligence (picture smart)
Interpersonal intelligence (people smart)
Naturalist intelligence (nature awareness smart)

(Notice that it spells the name of MILD KELVIN, who appears later in TOM's story. MILD KELVIN might help you to remember the ten intelligences.)

No-one completely understands how it all works, but we can use the theories very effectively in learning and teaching. By simply making sure that whatever you want to remember, or want someone else to remember, has somehow stimulated each intelligence, the brain will store a memory under that heading. More memories under more headings equals longer and stronger memories.

While you are reading this book, be aware that the information will be noticed and stored by different aspects of your 'smart-ness'. You will: look for rhythm, timing, tone and flow (music/rhythm smart), reflect and think about it (self smart), reason with logic (logic/reasoning smart), follow the story (story smart), imagine your senses being stimulated by the experiences in the story (sense smart), your emotions will be stirred up because you like some things and not others (feeling smart), read the words (word smart), look at the pictures and create your own mental images from the words used (picture smart), like TOM you will probably share what you learn with others (people smart), and finally, you will relate to aspects of nature mentioned in the story (nature smart). And all this will happen even if you aren't thinking about it. Amazing isn't it?

Later in this book we will return to these theories, but for the moment, just relax, keep reading and let your sub-conscious absorb the information. Let it auTOMatically sort it all out and apply it to your life.

So, to take full advantage of the format used to create this book, I suggest:
1. Follow TOM's trail through the contents storyboard (p. 9)
2. Quickly skim through the whole book and make mental notes of all the headings and the parts that interest you
3. Read the whole book from front to back as written
4. Return to TOM's Toolkit (p. 79) to get tips on how to handle specific issues
5. Follow the contents storyboard often and read the book again. Both conscious and subconscious messages will be made doubly strong with repetition, repetition.
6. This may be radical, but actually *use the techniques* to create the relationships and results you want in your life! What a concept! Oops... sorry. Sarcasm. But it's often the part that gets forgotten. Nothing actually changes until we choose to do something different.

So... let's take a look at how this mythical character called TOM could help improve your relationships and your life.

2

TOM and the Mountain

TOM is one of those intriguing sorts of guys – we all know and envy one – who seems to always get what he wants. He's Trusting and trustworthy, has clear Objectives and is always brimming with Motivation. Not only that, the people around TOM seem to Trust him, they seem to understand his and their own Objectives and are always Motivated to work with him on whatever he is currently up to. How is it that these three personal attributes work so well for him? No matter what he attempts to do in his life, he and the people around him are usually successful. Let's follow him on one of his adventures...

 One day, after weeks of careful planning, TOM sets off to climb a mountain. He knows he will have to have self-belief and *Trust* in his abilities and in his level of commitment to the task. He has a clear vision that inspires him to set specific and motivating *Objectives* and his *Motivation* to reach the top is... well... he's not really sure. His mate Ralph has promised to buy him a new pair of hiking boots if he makes it, 'But TOM thinks, 'that can't be the only reason I'm going.' He's really pumped up, but can't really understand why. Maybe there's more to a journey than just the steps you take. Perhaps he will learn more than just how far it is to the top. Already his mind is to-ing and fro-ing with all the possibilities.

Everyone agrees with TOM!

'Could it be that sometimes you only need a lot of trust and a vision of clear, inspirational objectives?' he wonders. 'Maybe the objectives can be motivating enough on their own without adding a reward. Maybe you only need a motivating reward or some sort of penalty if the trust is too low and the objectives don't excite you.' TOM considers that this might be just as much a mental and emotional journey as a physical one.

Patsy's PEAs

 As TOM steps from the train onto the platform he is acutely aware that he is the only person getting off at this station. He hands his spent ticket to the ticket collector and pushes through the rickety old wooden gate and finds himself on the outskirts of a small village.

To his left is a winding country road which disappears into a forest of old oak trees about a hundred metres from the station. Immediately to his right, only 30 centimetres from his right shoulder, he is greeted by a wide warm smile on the face of a short, grey-haired, old woman. Her hair is neatly tied back under a starched white cap and she is sitting behind a white picket fence just inside the front gate of her cottage. In front of her is a clean and sparklingly shiny stainless steel bowl perched on an equally clean and shiny counter. She's wearing a spotless white apron and her tiny gnarled hands are deftly shelling peas into the bowl. Above her head is suspended a canvas banner which simply proclaims: *'Patsy's Peas'*.

'How strange' he thinks. 'No other product, just peas. I don't think I've ever seen a pea shop before', he muses. But her face is kind, her eyes are bright and... 'Try one?' she says, looking at

TOM with raised eyebrows and offering him a gloved hand on which sits one large, round, fresh and delicious looking pea.
'Sorry?' he says, a little startled. He takes a small step back.
'Would you like to try one of these lovely green peas?' she repeats in more detail. But before he has a chance to answer, she begins to elaborate on all the reasons she likes peas... how good they are for you, how they are grown, the best way to shell them, the right water temperature to cook them in... TOM remembers very little of the content of the conversation after that. He is mesmerised by her banter and enthusiasm, but one thing sticks firmly in his mind:

'The PEA can teach you a lot about trust,' she says in a bold, sweeping statement. 'What do you mean by that?' TOM replies quizzically. 'The 'P' stands for Persona.' TOM looks confused. 'Let's go back a step and I'll explain.

You have an inbuilt mechanism that I call a *Trust Meter*. It's this auTOMatic measuring device that moves forward or back depending on the trust messages you receive from others. And I and everyone else have a trust meter too. Our level of trust in you is dependent on the messages you give us. We all have different levels of trust in people depending on the different experiences we have with them.

Part of the Trust Meter is also focussed internally, figuring out whether we trust ourselves enough to do one thing or another. Some people call it Self Belief. But let's talk about your trust in others first.

The thing that initially gets your trust meter to move is someone's Persona – how they look, how they dress, how they speak, how they act – they are all aspects of what you see as their persona. I'm guessing that what encouraged you to come over and talk to me in the first place had something to do with my persona.'

'Er… well… yes, I think so. You looked like a nice person, your apron was clean, your peas looked fresh, your metal bowl and counter looked… um… professional, I guess.'

'That's it! All those things make the trust meter move a little bit and they add up to give you a more complete picture of whether or not you think this is someone you could trust. I'm not saying you trusted me completely at that point, but the meter moved enough to get you to talk to me and maybe try my peas.'

TOM is pleased. He notices that he is starting to trust her a bit more because at last she is beginning to make sense!

'So… would you like to try one?'

TOM once again looks at the pea, plucks it eagerly from Patsy's hand, and devours it instantly. It is delicious. Small but delicious.

'And so now the second part of the trust process kicks in – the 'E' for Effectiveness. If my sales patter is effective at convincing you to try the pea (and it was) and if the pea is effective i.e. it tastes good and starts to satisfy your hunger (and it did) the trust meter moves again and you will probably trust me a little more.'
'You're right!' enthuses TOM. 'I was just thinking that it was so nice, I'm going to buy some to eat while I'm walking today. I guess I must trust you and your peas a little more.'

By now TOM is curious to hear the rest of the trust lesson. 'So… what about the 'A'?'

'Well, if you think back a few minutes there was a point at which you seemed a little nervous and could have walked away when I became a bit over-enthusiastic. And I might have thought you were a little crazy for not appreciating my peas. But I needed to *Accept* that you weren't as excited about my product as I was. And the ways of a little old lady are probably nothing like the ways of a young man.'

'OK, now let's see if I get this. If someone's *Persona* indicates that I might be able to trust them, I actually do start to trust them, just a little. And if their *Effectiveness* is also obvious and they are actually getting the job done – whatever that job is – I will probably trust them a little more. And if they show me *Acceptance* – accepting that I am doing my best to understand them, then Trust will more than likely start to grow. How's that?'

'Pretty good,' says Patsy, 'but here's a short version that might be easier to remember:

If you look like you can do it, and you are doing it well, and you don't judge me for the way I do it… I'll probably trust you.

Or from the other direction…

If I look like I can do it, I am doing it well, and I accept you for the way you do it… you'll probably trust me.'

'OK,' she continues, 'let's recap and add something that will help you make sense of this whole trust thing. We've said that this invisible trust meter measures the level of trust we have in ourselves or someone else (or a company, product, team…). What if this trust meter is driven by a set of personal ground rules? If a ground rule is matched, the trust meter moves forward; if it is broken, it moves backwards. I look OK, it moves forward a little. I stand too close, it breaks a ground rule you have, and it moves back. I smile and I'm nice to you (accept you the way you are) and it moves forward again. We are constantly matching and breaking other people's ground rules – it's all part of building trust. The more we stay within someone's ground rules, the more they will trust us, and the same applies to trust in ourselves. We set up a list of ground rules for ourselves (often called commitments) and the more we keep within these rules the more our self-belief, confidence and trust in ourselves grows.'

TOM needs to get going, but he really appreciates what Patsy and her peas have taught him. He buys a huge bag of them to munch along the way. The next train arrives and this time there are plenty of people flooding from the platform and forming an orderly queue at Patsy's stand. He thanks her, waves goodbye and heads off down the road toward the oak trees. Just as he reaches the corner, he notices a small track veering off to the right. An old wooden sign at the roadside simply says:

He has been told that the track will take him via the village to the wonderful VISTA at the top of the mountain.

'Mmm… VISTA via the Village' he thinks. 'That's probably a great way to remember it.' And off he strides into the forest mumbling 'VISTA Via the Village, VISTA Via the Village, VISTA Via the Village' as he walks.

The distant VISTA and the 3 E's of Life
TOM has set out with quite a lot of *expectations* of how this trip
will unfold, what *events* will happen along the way and how he
will *evaluate* his progress.

(1) From 'The Enlightened Response'
*'Our lives, viewed through our senses and our own perception filters,
are really nothing else except EXPECTATIONS, EVENTS and
EVALUATIONS. It is a continual process we experience every minute
of every day. Our lives only exist in our thoughts. Without our
thoughts about these 3 E's of Life, do we really have a life?'*

Our thoughts can only be about 3 spaces in time:
* Thoughts about the future – what is going to happen or could
happen (Expectations)
* Thoughts about the present - what is happening (Events)
* Thoughts about the past - what happened (Evaluations)

All of his *expectations* are based on how things look and feel
when he visualises his objective – excited and confident as he
imagines standing at the top and enjoying the VISTA.

As each *event* comes and goes he evaluates them compared to his
expectations, and then sets new expectations based on these
evaluations – the track is easier than expected, he speeds up and
expects to get to the top earlier.

His final *evaluations* are based on a) the original expectations he
had as he planned and began his trip, b) the evaluations of
events along the way and c) how he feels at the end when he
reaches his visualised objective. Arriving early will exceed his
expectations and he will evaluate his success even more
favourably than first expected.

Everyone agrees with TOM!

He is deep in thought now as he picks up pace and lengthens his stride. 'Maybe we need to carefully consider the expectations we have,' he says out loud. He remembers an old Arabic proverb that effectively translates to: 'Trust in God, but tie up your camels anyway.' It was an old friend of his father who he had first heard it from. He had gone on to explain, 'Expect the best, but realise that this is life. If we expect the unexpected there is no need to be surprised when it happens. There is also no need to focus on or picture details of failure, only to know that it is a possibility. This touch of reality thinking could possibly save you a lot of heartache.' As TOM started this project he had clearly visualised what it would look and feel like when he was successful. He now repeats the wise words of his dad's friend and although he doesn't focus on it, he is conscious that the world will continue to turn even if he doesn't realise his vision.

Through small gaps between the trees he can see the peak of the mountain far off in the distance and in his 'mind's eye'[1] he can see himself standing proudly at the summit. Over the last few weeks this same *vision* has **inspired** him to get everything done: buy equipment, get fit, plan the route, and lots of other *specific* details that needed to be checked and finalised. He even calculated how much *time* each stage would take and as the day drew nearer he had ticked these items off his list and felt good as he *assessed* his progress. He is proud of what he has achieved to get this far. He glances again at the far off **VISTA** and it seems to inject a spring into his step.

WIIFU Motivation

Many years earlier, TOM had been told a story about a small furry creature that inhabited this tiny patch of forest. The animal was known as a WIIFU and legend had it that actually catching a glimpse of this shy creature would bring good fortune. In a way

22

it meant that seeing the WIIFU had a built in reward. He began thinking that this was just like life. If we can see the WIIFU (the

 What's In It For Us), then we will be motivated to do whatever is necessary to achieve the result we want. And the 'Us' refers to all those involved. If I get something out of it and you get something out of it and it's good for the company or the family or the environment... The more everybody gets out of it, the more motivating it is going to be.

TOM thinks about all the benefits of achieving his objectives. He once again imagines how he will feel when he rounds the last bend, climbs the last rock and takes in the glorious VISTA before him. He ponders on how it will be good for his health and self esteem. He imagines telling his friends and work colleagues of his success and how it might inspire them to do something exciting and adventurous and how that will be good for their health and self esteem. He pictures all the new experiences he is going to have along the way, all the benefits for him and others, all the WIIFU's. Although he doesn't actually see the legendary WIIFU, he spends quite some time thinking about his own WIIFU's... (so in his own way he really does see it) and he starts walking faster.

Meanwhile, sitting safely at home, TOM's mate Ralph thinks TOM has no chance of succeeding, but then, Ralph always thinks like that. No need to describe the picture in his head! (But you just saw it didn't you?

The Lemon Man

Twenty minutes of walking brings TOM to a picturesque village straddled over a crystal clear stream. There seems to be hardly 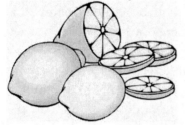 anyone about, but as he follows the track down a lane he suddenly emerges into a bustling town square and finds himself pushing through a crowded country market.

Above all the noise and hubbub he hears a clear, distinctive voice calling, 'Lemons, lemons, big juicy lemons! Buy your sweet juicy fresh lemons and lemonade here!' As he listens to this voice, and hears the **words** being used to describe these big, juicy, fresh lemons he begins to see **pictures** of them in his mind and his mouth starts to water. By the time he tracks down the voice and actually sees the man and the lemon stand, he experiences the **feelings** of his mouth salivating with the expectation of drinking cool, refreshing lemonade. He decides to take **action** and makes a bee-line for the lemon stall.

The Lemon Man (real name: MILD KELVIN) has a large wooden table set up with a huge set of antique scales, a massive pile of lemons and every lemon product imaginable. There's lemon jam, lemon butter, lemon pie, lemon curd, lemon cakes, lemon soap, lemon air freshener, lemon detergent... and of course, big, icy cold bottles of lemonade. The Lemon Man has a happy, lilting, almost musical voice that makes TOM feel good.

The voice actually makes him feel like he wants to buy the lemons. The scales remind him that there are two sides to every communication – the practical side and the emotional side. The *task* of selling the lemons could be done almost completely without emotion – just a mechanical transaction between seller and buyer. But because the happy lemon man with the musical, lilting voice makes TOM *feel* good, he is much more likely to buy lemons, then buy more lemons, then buy lemons more often… and then encourage his friends to buy, buy more, buy more often…

TOM hears the man talking about the 'big juicy lemons', sees the shiny bright lemons, feels the smooth dimpled skin, smells the sweet fragrance of the cut lemons and feels the tingle on his tongue as he tastes the tangy lemon juice… He is so impressed with this amazing lemon experience, he begins shouting to other passers by, 'Come and see these amazing lemons, taste the lemonade! Try the incredible lemon soap…!'

…and now, every time TOM hears the word 'lemon', this vivid string of memories immediately springs to mind. Why? Maybe it is because the lemons represent a complete learning experience for him. First he **hears** about the lemons (and has a 25% chance of remembering them), he **sees** the lemons and the stand and the lemonade (now a 50% chance of remembering), he physically experiences the lemons by **touching, smelling, tasting** and **buying** the lemons (now a 75% chance of remembering) and as he leaves the lemon man, he tells another walker coming the other way about the '…lovely lemons, lemons, big juicy lemons! You can buy sweet, juicy, fresh, lemons and lemonade just around the bend!' He literally **teaches** them about the lemons (…and now 100% chance of remembering).

(Is your mouth watering? Can you taste the lemons?)

TOM was reminded too of something he had read about how the human mind and body responds to communication. It was all very scientific, but the simple version was…

Words produce **pictures,** pictures produce **feelings,** feelings produce **action.**

'So…' he ponders, 'If I want to change my **actions**, I have to **feel** something, so I have to create the right **picture** to produce the feeling and I have to use the right **words** to trigger the most effective picture.' He resolves to give more thought to the words he uses. 'I'm learning lots of stuff,' he thinks to himself. 'Maybe I can use my words and pictures and feelings and actions to remember it all. If I hear it, see it, get all my senses involved with it and tell other people about it, maybe it will all stay stored in my brain somewhere.'

MAL and BJ

TOM works his way to the edge of the town square, around the corner of the town hall, down another narrow lane and picks up  the trail again. In no time he is away from the houses of the village, crossing fields and entering the forest where the terrain becomes steeper and the road a little rougher. An hour goes by, and then two and at the end of a particularly long straight, rocky stretch, TOM becomes thirsty once again. As luck would have it, on the very next bend the track crosses a narrow country road and passes a small country pub. TOM stops, buys a drink and sits at a table in the corner.

At the bar there are two men talking. TOM can't help but overhear their loud conversation, and picks up that their names are MAL and BJ. A short way along the bar stands another man with a huge nose.

'Hey big nose,' BJ shouts, 'don't turn around too fast or you'll knock us all down with that thing!' MAL warns him to stop, but BJ thinks it's a great joke. Suddenly the 'big nose' guy, reaching breaking point, comes running down the bar and punches BJ on his nose.

TOM, watching the whole scene, can easily see what's going on, but BJ is unrepentant. 'Did ya see that?', he yells. 'That guy hit me, for no reason at all. All I was doing was having a little joke!'

'Mmm' TOM thinks. 'Can't he see how he *made* that happen?'

What 4 Feedback
As if echoing TOM's thoughts, MAL decides to offer BJ some advice. It's always a risky business offering someone advice, especially a friend, but TOM really admires the way MAL delivers it. First, he really listens to BJ's point of view, he labels his comments differently by calling it **feedback**, and then MAL does something TOM thinks is truly inspired – he actually *asks* BJ if he is 'open to receiving some feedback'. TOM remembers many times when people – family, friends, colleagues – have dumped a whole cocktail of facts, information, advice and opinion on him that he hadn't really invited or expected.

Asking permission is probably a very good idea TOM surmises. He has heard the word feedback many times before and has always thought that it meant something like 'bad news'. It seemed like it had to be delivered with an angry, sarcastic, disappointed or condescending tone in the voice and only given to people when they had to be told that they were doing something wrong.

But MAL speaks to BJ in a clear and neutral sort of way. It sounds balanced and has two obvious features – it is factual and friendly – and it seems to come in four distinct packages. First he tells him:

What happened, which simply tells BJ the behaviour MAL has observed. There is no sound of criticism or judgment in his voice, no opinions or advice, just three clear facts.

'You spoke too loud, you said things that some people would call inappropriate and you didn't move quick enough to get away from the guy when he came after you.' Then he tells him:

What happened next, which TOM thinks is really useful. So many times people have told him things – the *What happened* – and he has thought, 'So what?', because he hasn't seen the relevance or what it had to do with him. He has even answered with something like, 'Well, what's wrong with that?!' The *What happened next* often gives the main reason for the feedback in the first place. TOM thinks, 'Maybe it's not the *what happened* that is the main problem, but the *what happened next* as a result of *what happened* first.'

TOM listens while MAL tells BJ:

'What happened next was, Mr Big Nose heard you, he was upset by what you said, he punched you and now you have a sore nose'.

BJ was listening intently as he had the feeling that MAL was going to offer his ideas on how to change or improve the situation; the:

What now. MAL suggests several things BJ can do. TOM thinks these are quite sensible options in the circumstances. Things like... only looking at and talking to MAL and other people in the bar, keeping his voice down and restricting his conversation to more general comments about miscellaneous body parts. BJ doesn't seem altogether convinced that this course of action will keep him out of trouble, but he listens as MAL tells him the:

What for. These seem to be some of the main reasons for doing things differently. TOM thinks this is something that is often lacking when people give him feedback. Again he thinks, 'The people around me can be quite good at telling me where I am going wrong, what problems it is causing and even what I could do to change it, but often what is missing is the reward. It seems like there could be some quite valid benefits for BJ changing his behaviour.' TOM listened as MAL broke it down into 3 key words and 3 clear messages...

1. **Drinking**. MAL and BJ would be able to remain in the bar and finish their drinks (without being attacked by the now angry man with the big nose!).
2. **Safety.** The colour and shape of BJ's own nose would remain the same as when he first entered the bar (instead of being red and swollen!).
3. **Entertainment.** They could be entertained by the boxing match on the television behind the bar (instead of BJ being caught up in his own private and painful boxing match and becoming part of the entertainment!).

BJ seems to have absorbed at least some of MAL's feedback. He keeps quiet for a while and the three men go back to their drinking. But eventually the temptation is too great for BJ and he whispers to MAL. 'Man, look at the size of that snoz! If he breathes in again, we'll all suffocate!' Big Nose's ears prick up and again he comes running down the bar and punches BJ.

And TOM thinks to himself, 'Well I guess he didn't mean to make it happen, but he certainly assisted it along.' He had heeded the first two pieces of feedback from MAL – he had kept his voice down... and he was only talking to MAL, but that nose! BJ couldn't steer his mind or his comments away from it.

Once again MAL offers his 'factual and friendly feedback'. It is the exact same message. Consistency might win through in the end.

BJ now seems to have learned his lesson and stands passively at the bar, nursing his swollen nose and talking quietly to his mate MAL.

Just as calm begins to descend over the scene, at the other end of the bar another loudmouth is telling some guy what a huge ugly nose he has. MAL turns to his mate and says, 'Come on, there's going to be trouble, let's go.' BJ protests at having to leave the excitement, MAL gives in and they stay and watch the 'discussion'. Well, the discussion becomes an argument and the argument turns into a fight and again MAL suggests they go. But again BJ refuses as he wants to 'see what happens'. Soon there are five in the fight, then ten, then fifteen... and eventually the two curious onlookers get caught up in the brawl, chairs are broken over their heads and they are carted off to hospital.

Sitting at a safe distance from all the action, TOM recounts the events of the past few minutes. 'Mmm...' he thinks, 'How did all that happen? It was pretty obvious that BJ earned his first punch on the nose – he certainly **made** it happen. And the second time?

Not so obvious, but he was definitely responsible for **assisting** the outcome by ignoring some of the feedback. And finally, didn't he simply ignore all the warning signs and **let** things take their course without taking responsibility for removing himself from the situation? His reaction, like many of us, was to blame something or someone for the way things turned out, or to justify why he did what he did. I guess that's why MAL calls him BJ.'

TOM reflects for a moment on just how we Make, Assist or Let things happen in our lives. 'I think we really do have Response-Ability over every aspect of our lives – especially our responses to what happens. It seems that MAL understood this. Our expectations are often the catalyst for many of the events of our lives and we need to understand that we are all responsible, if not for the events, then at least for the evaluations of those events. It's actually our thoughts and expectations that often produce the behaviours that Make things happen. And sometimes it's not so obvious, but we still do things that Assist the outcome to turn out the way it does. And if we don't concede that we Make things happen or Assist things to happen, then there really is only one more option – we Let things happen.'

TOM is on a roll now and he keeps thinking... 'We all have things that just happen to us, and we can either see them as 'good' things or 'bad' things. We can *let* them affect the way we think, act or feel or we can recognize that it is a 'cause and effect' universe, virtually controlled and governed by how we think. Our lives really are just in our thoughts. But how we react to what happens is far more important than what actually happens.'

Everyone agrees with TOM!

'We even have a major part to play in the creation of other's perceptions of us – we make them think certain ways about us because of our actions, we assist the confirmation of those perceptions, again with our actions or what we say, and we let these erroneous perceptions persist without trying to influence or challenge them.'

TOM also thinks about how effective MAL has been at getting BJ to listen to him. He reflects on some of his own past conversations with people and realises how quickly he often judges others for being poor listeners when the finger of responsibility could more easily be pointed at himself. 'Maybe I can learn from MAL' he thinks. 'It's true that I could be a better listener if I…

1. **Focus** on what people were saying
2. **Reflect** back to them that I am listening (by nodding, responding, questioning, interacting, acknowledging…)
3. **Summarise** back to them my understanding of what they are saying.

But equally I could make it much easier for others to listen to me if I…

1. **Give** *Key Words* and simple clear messages to focus on.
2. **Invite** reflection, reaction and response so I can tell if they are listening.
3. **Ask** them to summarise so I can gauge understanding.

TOM is enjoying his little interlude in the pub and learning a lot about response-ability, feedback and communication, but the road beckons – and just like the skill of listening, he will have to stay focussed if he is going to get the result he wants.

The Triple 'A' Bridge

Immediately across the road from the pub, the track disappears into thick forest, but within a hundred yards TOM is confronted  with a challenge. Across a deep ravine is a long rickety suspension bridge slung lazily and somewhat precariously several hundred feet above a raging river. Someone has erected a rough sign out of bush timber. 'TRIPLE 'A' BRIDGE' it says, and as he takes a closer look he can see why. The central framework of ropes actually forms three distinct 'A' shapes. While *assessing* whether or not it is safe enough to cross, TOM notices that, about half way across, some of the small logs that form the walkway are rotten, broken or even missing.

Standing with him and also wondering whether or not to cross, is another trekker. TOM is staring at the bridge, but his mind has wandered ahead toward solving the problem. 'I'm going to need help with this,' he thinks. 'I wonder what this guy is like. He looks OK, but I wonder if we can work together.' TOM has never seen him before, doesn't know what sort of person he is or how he likes to do things, but if they are going to work together he thinks to himself that the faster he gets to know him, the more chance they have of succeeding. He sees the bridge as a metaphor – a sort of symbol that represents another idea or concept. He considers the idea that communication is like building bridges between people. Sometimes you need to build a bridge to get to someone, but also make sure it lands where they are, not where you want them to be. To build trust with them, somehow you have to find things in common, because we tend to like and trust people who are like ourselves... and you have to build the trust before you set objectives... and you have to find something that motivates you both to get the job done. 'Mmm...' he thinks. 'It all sounds very familiar.'

They exchange the usual pleasantries, talk about their respective journeys and together begin to **Assess** the broken bridge. They have a lot in common – especially the need to get across the river. TOM knows he gets very task-focussed in these situations and tends to want to control things. The trekker seems pretty easy going and seems willing to support TOM who already has some ideas of what they could do. Although neither of them says anything about it, they seem to trust each other enough to make a start. Their shared objectives seem clear – fix the bridge – but the methods and specific steps aren't yet. How will they actually do it? What tools will they use? Who will do what? How long will it take?

They begin formulating a plan and quickly learn that they are both motivated by a similar goal. They both have a mountain to climb... but it's not the same mountain. TOM supposes that this is often the case when people work together. It's not vitally important that they have exactly the same objective, but there needs to be enough common ground to motivate them both to move in the same direction. There has to be sufficient What's In It For Me, in the What's In It For Us, to get us going.

Trust, objectives, motivation... it all seems to be there. They **Agree** and get started.

The two empty the contents of their backpacks on the ground to see what tools they have that could help. Nothing seems quite what they need. TOM has a rusty old pen-knife with a couple of weird attachments – file, pliers and a tiny saw, but they aren't really up to the job of cutting new logs for the bridge. The other trekker has only a small folding shovel. They are hardly equipped for a major engineering project, but then TOM is suddenly struck by a brilliant idea. 'Why don't we **Adapt** your shovel?' he says, "by sharpening the blade with the file on my penknife? Then we can use it as an axe to cut the logs to fix the bridge.'

In no time they have their problem solved – shovel sharpened, logs cut and bridge repaired – and they are once again on their way to their individual mountains. TOM bids farewell to his temporary workmate and once again strides off purposefully into the forest. He walks at a steady pace, but his mind is racing.

'I knew trust, objectives and motivation were important, but I guess I didn't realise just how large a part they play in getting things done – especially when you have to work with other people. It's like building bridges between people – the three elements need to be there right from the start, so you can get a strong agreement ...and then they still have to be there if you need to adapt the agreement ...and then you have to assess that they are still all there when you achieve what you agreed on. If they are all there at the end, and especially if you get the result that motivated you to make the agreement, then it is imperative that you *apply the motivating factor*! If you acknowledge yourself and others for the achievement, you'll feel great, and then you'll probably be motivated enough to... make more agreements. Mmm...' he thinks, 'maybe that's why I like working with some people more than others. Maybe that's why I feel motivated to work more for some bosses and less for others. If all the elements are there...'

Everyone agrees with TOM!

TOM ponders on all this as he walks. He thinks about different people in his life, especially the ones he has enjoyed working with and, it dawns on him that there is a very obvious common thread – he liked, respected and especially… trusted them. It felt good to be around them. They always had the task in mind, but they never lost sight of how TOM felt about what he was doing. But even more important than that… they set him up to be and feel successful! Somehow they always seemed to organize things so that he achieved his part of whatever they had set out to do. Or even if he didn't succeed, they had always made him feel good about what he had done. 'But…' he wonders, 'does this work the same with everyone?'

The Behavioural Blender

As he winds his way along the track he reflects on how strange

it is that all the people he has encountered so far – Patsy and her trusty peas, the Lemon Man, MAL, BJ and the trekker – have all seen the world a little differently to him. Those thoughts lead him to ponder… he likes to ponder… on his own view of the world and how even that is not constant. He remembers the scales on the Lemon Man's table. They remind him that sometimes he is only interested in the <u>task</u> – he is *outspoken* and single-minded, focused on getting things done and being in **Control**; and yet sometimes he is *quieter*, methodical and wants to analyze everything, see the detail and **Perfect** things. Sometimes he is only interested in how things <u>feel</u> – he is *outspoken*, full of fun, flits from one interest to another and wants to **Entertain** himself and others; and yet other times he is *quieter*, likes routine, is willing to flow along and do what anyone else wants and to **Mediate** and keep the peace. He also remembers that, when he is outspoken he tends to <u>tell</u> more than ask, and when he is quieter he tends to <u>ask</u> more than tell.

.TOM ponders on... 'It's like having at least four different pairs of eye glasses that you wear one pair at a time, or sometimes two at the same time, and they help you see the world and consequently behave in different ways... and it's like you carry them around in a big rucksack and bring them out and blend them together depending on how you feel and what you're looking at.' (TOM also ponders if everyone else ponders like he ponders!)

The track becomes steeper again the further he gets from the river and on rounding a sharp bend the trail suddenly bursts through a patch of thick undergrowth and he finds himself dumped on a round grassy clearing at the edge of a long stretch of gravel road. It must be a sort of meeting place for trekkers because there are about twenty of them sitting on folding chairs and around tables scattered around a small fruit juice hut.

He hasn't had anything to drink since he left MAL and BJ at the pub, so he steps up to the counter and orders a tantalizing sounding blend of apple, carrot, banana and strawberry juice. The girl asks him if he wants ice. When he answers that he does, she chips a large piece off a bluish looking ice block in a freezer in the corner. 'Where did you get that?' he asks. 'Oh the boss goes up every day and brings down a chunk from the iceberg in the lake.' TOM has never seen an iceberg and starts to get excited about the next stage of the climb. But for now he is intrigued by the giant blender rumbling and whirring on the counter in front of him.

The new juice starts out looking quite yellow... and then goes through a brief pinky stage and finally the carrot colour starts to dominate. Watching the blades in the blender whiz noisily around and the fruits slowly losing their own individuality, he begins to think about personalities and behavioural styles and how they are also a blend – a blend of many different thoughts, feelings... and the behaviours that follow them.

He even thinks that sometimes these different styles or personalities combine in different proportions to give many different variations, flavours and colours. If at any particular moment the assertive and outspoken **Control** style blends with the quieter, analytical, detail conscious **Perfect** style, you might have someone who gets the job done and makes sure it is right, but maybe doesn't consider the feelings of others involved and will perhaps be more work focussed than fun focussed. And then again, if the **Entertain** style blends with the **Control** style, you will probably get someone who is very outspoken, gets on with the job, but has a real laugh along the way. A **Mediate** style blended with just about anyone else will probably have the effect of calming the other down and helping them to see everyone else's viewpoint, but they may not be as quick at getting a job done or forthcoming with ideas and initiatives.

He begins to think how flexible and changeable it all is. In fact the combinations will be infinite because every person has a bit of every style, and more importantly, depending on their mood and the situation, the blend will be different. TOM certainly doesn't enjoy people categorising him, but he realizes how easily he sometimes does it to others. He will see them be aggressive, maybe even only for a few seconds, but then somehow he always sees them that way. Maybe all he is really seeing is a blending stage – a moment when this person is changing their glasses.

Thinking back to the Triple 'A' bridge, he wonders if that's why he got on well with the trekker. 'At that moment, maybe I had had my control and entertain glasses on and was full of energy and creative ideas, and the trekker had had his mediate and perfect glasses on, so he was willing to go along with my ideas, focus on the finer details and work methodically to get the job done. If, say, we both had been wearing control glasses, we might have clashed – both wanting to be in control at the same time. Or if we both had our entertain glasses on, perhaps we would have joked around, had lots of ideas and had a lot of fun, but might not have had enough focus to actually get on with making a decision and achieving a result.'

Just as he is contemplating all these intricacies of human personality, he hears a strange chant behind him. Two small children are playing 'paddy-cake' and as their hands clap together they are singing 'Con-trol, per-fect, en-ter-tain and me-di-ate... Con-trol, per-fect, en-ter-tain and me-di-ate... Con-tr...'

He has a lot of weird thoughts spinning in his head as he downs his juice and sets off once again towards the mountain. The air becomes cooler as he climbs and the track winds and zigzags up steep rocky slopes. Still pondering on Behavioural Blends and how each different combination will see their world slightly differently, he carefully edges his way around a huge boulder at the top of a long strenuous climb.

Everyone agrees with TOM!

The Values Iceberg

Stretched out in front of him, several hundred feet below, is a huge alpine lake walled in by mountains on two sides.

Immediately below, a stream is gurgling and rushing away from the still deep waters. At the far end of the lake, perhaps a couple of miles away, he can just make out the sheer bluish-white ice walls of a glacier. It is a beautifully magical scene, like something from a Swiss calendar, but what really takes his attention is a gigantic island of ice floating at the very centre of the lake. An iceberg! All his life TOM has dreamed of one day seeing one of these masterpieces of nature.

He studies the iceberg intently, marveling at its massive size and imposing bulk, and then also notices how the sharp edges of its massive walls fade and disappear into the icy blue water below. There is much more below the surface than above it. Somewhere from the deep recesses of his memory he dredges up the figures of '...80% of an iceberg is below the surface'. Echoes of an old and much loved school teacher he guesses, but again it sets him thinking. 'Icebergs are a lot like people.'

All we clearly see of icebergs is what shows above the surface... and all we really know of other people is what they are prepared to leave on display. We make decisions about them – who they are, what they think and what they value in their lives – based mainly on the behaviours we see. 'What if...' TOM thinks, 'What if all behaviours, theirs and ours, are instigated by the thoughts and beliefs we hold just below the surface? And what if those thoughts and beliefs are powered by something even deeper than that? ...our Values.'

'That would explain a whole lot about why other people don't see things my way,' he mumbles to himself out loud. 'They physically can't!' TOM had heard that scientists have discovered that, similar as they may be in size and basic structure, our brains all function slightly differently. 'I didn't inherit the same genes and DNA as anyone else, and my upbringing, even if I was brought up in the same house, was vastly different to anyone else's. So when with exasperation I say to someone, 'Can't you see that?!?' the answer has got to be, 'No! I can't possibly behave exactly the same way as you because deep down my **values** have been shaped differently to yours... causing me to think and believe differently to you... which causes me to act differently to you... which shapes my values again...'

TOM's head is full of the adventures of the day so far... Patsy's Peas... the Lemon Man... MAL and BJ in the pub... the Triple 'A' Bridge... the Behavioural Blender... the Values Iceberg...

Dazed with all his new realizations he stumbles along the lakeside track that wanders higher and higher until he finds his boots crunching across the smooth hard ice of the glacier. At this point the way is less obvious, the trail is fuzzy and indistinct and there are numerous possibilities. He follows what he thinks is the most likely route, but his steps are tentative... cautious... He isn't happy. TOM raises his eyes from the slippery ice to discover a huge black storm cloud has gathered overhead. A violent gust of wind hits him from behind. He staggers, regains his footing and as he turns to face the blast of icy cold air he feels his face stinging with the onslaught of gritty balls of sleet. His heart is racing. His body trembles with fear. He begins to run in blind panic... and then...

Pause Button

...a voice seems to call from somewhere deep inside TOM's head... 'Remember the *Pause Button* TOM.'

'What...? Where...? Who said...?' he asks his imaginary questioner ...and then he begins to remember something a friend had taught him many years ago. Her son had been in a fight when he was picked on by a bully at school. Unfortunately the young boy, and not the bully, had been the one caught and punished and he really couldn't see the fairness in it. Then the mother had taught the boy how to use the *Pause Button* before jumping into action. She demonstrated on an old CD player that, 'Just like a noisy, loud CD can be instantly paused, so too can the noisy, loud voices in our heads be paused. These are the ones that yell at us to do something as a response to fear or anger. And often they are the same thing – fear and anger all mixed up in an ugly ball,' she had said. 'If you get into one of those situations again, just stop, mentally apply the *Pause Button* to whatever is going on, and suddenly everything will become much clearer. Instead of panicking and doing something rash or foolish, or that will only make things worse, you will now have time to choose an *enlightened response* – one that has more light shining on it and is easy to see when you *pause* to think – the sort of thing that someone wise would do.'

That whole story flashes through TOM's mind in seconds. He stops, takes a deep breath, mentally applies his Pause Button, glances quickly around, and with what seems like new eyes he notices a small rock overhang just to the side of the trail. He dives into the tiny sheltered cave and calmly sits out the storm.

Surprisingly, as violent and unexpected as it is, it only rages for maybe ten minutes and disappears down the valley as quickly as it had come. TOM steps out into bright sunshine and tries to make sense of the last few minutes.

Whadayawant? – Don't turn left at the black stump
As he stands there scratching his head and wondering what to do next, he hears the sound of footsteps on ice. He scans the  horizon trying to gauge which way the steps are coming from, but he sees nothing. Then, just as he begins to think he might be going mad, the top of a head appears over the brow of a small ice hummock. The face becomes visible and then shoulders, until the complete figure of a girl in a skirt, carrying a short, black walking stick and wearing a backpack can be seen striding toward him but at a complete right-angle to the direction TOM is heading. TOM asks the girl for directions to the mountain summit. At first it seems she hasn't heard his question as she responds with a loud and raucous, 'WHADAYAWANT? He cautiously repeats his plea… and she begins…

'It's easy', she says. 'You go straight up the hill here for about two hundred metres until you get to a big black tree stump with three trails heading away from it. <u>Don't turn left there!</u> If you carry on up the hill for about another three hundred metres, you'll get to an ice cave. Now… if you get there, turn back because you've gone too far. Back at the black stump you should have gone right. Of course, if you're coming back from the ice cave, the right track will be on your left. Forget that I said don't turn left as that only applies when you're heading up the hill toward the stump. Once you are on the right track you'll get down to a small stone bridge. Now a lot of people go across that bridge and up the hill veering left, but I wouldn't if I were you. I would... and... bi... ...ack.' But by now the girl's voice is trailing away as the whole time she has been talking she has continued walking and is now about fifty yards away down the hill and disappearing fast. 'How strange', he thinks. 'I was less confused before I asked her!'

TOM secretly wishes that more people would talk about what 'to' do rather than what 'not' to do. He has pictures in his head of turning left... then not turning left; of getting to an ice cave he shouldn't see and coming back to a place and turning left where he has been told not to turn left. 'How much simpler life would be,' he thinks, 'if people talked about what they want, rather than what they don't want.'

He is reminded of the Lemon Man and how the words about lemons produced pictures of lemons which triggered the feelings of actually sucking a lemon which caused the action that his mouth started watering long before he got to the lemon stall. 'This is similar, but in reverse,' he thinks. 'The young woman using words describing what I don't want (don't turn left) creates pictures of me being where I don't want to be (at the ice cave) which makes me feel something (frustrated and disappointed) which brings about the action of me standing around confused and not knowing where to go next.' He still needs some help.

What 4 Feedback (again)

His trek has been mostly easy so far – lots of new experiences,

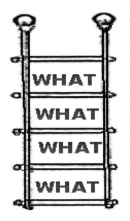 but nothing too frightening or challenging. The prospect of losing the path and fears of the ice moving under his feet makes him very uneasy. What he needs is some advice or a message from somewhere that he is on the right track. Again he thinks, 'This is just like life! Things go along smoothly for a while and I think I've got it all worked out, and then something happens to throw me off course. Ideally what I need at a point like this is a wise voice in my head whispering things like... 'Yes, you're on-course, keep going... No, off-course... a little left... yes, that's ok... On-course again...'

'I guess what I need is **feedback**,' he ponders again, thinking back to his time observing MAL and BJ in the pub. 'Isn't it funny how some people seem to get so upset about receiving feedback, and all worked up about giving it, when really it's just information to keep us on-course. Sure it is delivered in rough packages sometimes – with anger, guilt, expectations or sarcasm attached – but there is always a gift in there somewhere.'

He remembers getting a gift from his four-year old niece on his last birthday. She had spent ages doing her best to make it look pretty, but the skills didn't quite match the intention and, well... it was a mess. He also remembers that he absolutely adored the tiny gift inside and it was still valuable in spite of the wrapping.

'Feedback is like that.' he whispers to himself. 'I might not always like the wrapping, but if I look hard enough there will always be something inside that can teach me something. If it doesn't teach me something about myself, it will most definitely teach me something about someone else, and that's got to be valuable! Even if I only learn that the giver of the feedback is angry or sarcastic or just a poor communicator, that's got to be useful if I want to build a relationship with them or just get them to do something for me.

And it's up to me what I do with the information I receive. I could be a BJ and **Blame** them for making me angry and I could **Justify** my annoyance at what they had done or said to me OR... I could be a MAL and **Make** use of the information, have it **Assist** me to make choices and decisions and **Let** it guide me as to the best way to take Response-Ability.'

What TOM needs now is some **What 4 Feedback**, just like MAL gave BJ.

Just as he is looking for some inspiration, the track comes to an abrupt halt at the edge of a yawning crevasse. The sudden stop and overwhelming silence takes his breath away. A small chip of ice slides from the toe of his boot, rolls to the edge of the precipice and noiselessly disappears into the void. There is no sound for five or six whole seconds until... the click... click... chip... muffled sound of the falling ice bouncing off the walls floats up from the darkness below. 'That is feedback' he mumbles to himself. It is quite clearly saying not to go forward. But isn't it funny that sometimes no matter how loud, obvious or compelling the feedback might be, we still often choose to step off into a dark yawning black hole, somehow kidding ourselves that the feedback was inaccurate and 'everything will be fine'. Luckily TOM chooses to listen to this feedback and begins looking for an alternative route.

No track left or right. His way seems completely blocked. Just as he is contemplating the possible end of his trek and having to turn back, some feedback arrives in a most curious manner. About 50 feet away, suspended above the crevasse, sits a small blue and white bird chirping a sort of impatient two-note song. The call isn't loud, but it is certainly persistent. It seems to be saying, 'this-way, this-way… this-way, this-way…'

TOM backs away from the edge and makes his way along the crevasse towards the tiny messenger. As he draws closer he can see that, rather than being magically suspended above this massive ice-crack, the bird is perched on a ladder that has been laid purposefully across the gap.

The ladder seems quite robust and is secured with long steel spikes at each end. It takes four rungs to span the gap and on each rung the word **What** is hand-painted in bold letters on a small hanging metal sign. The first two are painted in red, the third blue and the last one in red. He figures that the blue one must have some slightly different significance – maybe he will find out when he gets there.

What happened
TOM takes a deep breath and tentatively reaches out until his foot touches the first rung. As his boot comes into contact with the metal and his weight settles onto it, he feels the rung roll under the sole of his boot and slip clunkily in its sockets. It gives him quite a fright. 'I wonder if anyone knows about this' he thinks. 'Perhaps there's a park ranger or maintenance man I can tell *What happened*.'

What happened next

TOM is also thinking about how the moving rung has scared him and how now he is quite fearful about the crossing. 'Is it safe?' he thinks. 'What will happen if it breaks?' He cautiously steps onto the second rung and decides he will have to tell the maintenance man *What happened next* – how the moving rung had made him feel and how it had hindered his progress. 'If I just tell him the problem,' he thinks, 'that mightn't be enough, as the fact that the rung is loose mightn't mean anything to him. But if I explain that the loose rung might cause someone to fall, that might make the difference that moves him to do something about it.'

What now

As he reaches the third rung, he notices a man standing just off to the right hand side of the ladder on the far side of the chasm. A small badge on his jacket identifies him as the Park Ranger.

'Everything OK?' he asks. TOM tells him *What happened* (about the unstable rung) and then *What happened next* (how it had made him fearful). Now he has reached the third rung – the *What now* part of the story – he glances back over his shoulder to the first two rungs and realises something important.

He sees the ladder as a sort of line through time and contemplates on the idea that all feedback is structured the same way. The **What 4** method of giving feedback follows the same line. The actual moment you give or receive feedback is always the *What now* point. That's why the *What now* sign is a different colour. From the *What now* point the giver and the receiver look back along this feedback line at *What happened*. They then progress logically along the line to talk about *What happened next*, because this is often far more important than what actually happened. The *What now* point is where you decide what and how to change things, if they're not working, or what and how to continue things if they are working.

The ranger listens to TOM's story, and he seems to agree that something needs to be done by someone, sometime; but he doesn't seem convinced it is urgent. As TOM stretches his foot forward onto the last rung, he is immediately aware of *what* it is *for* – it is the *What for* step in the process – the 'Why it's a good idea' part. 'And perhaps', he thinks, '…this is the most important part. Nothing happens in life unless we are motivated to do it. We never move forward unless we are pulled toward it (motivated by want or desire) or pushed into it (by fear or need). Without a strong *What for*, why would we ever want or need to do anything? I never change my behaviour just because someone else thinks it is a good idea. If I look deeply into it, I only really change my actions or behaviour if 'I' think it's a good idea and I can recognise the WIIFM (What's In It For Me). I may just be doing it so I don't get into trouble, but isn't that a WIIFM for me? A Benefit? The fact that I will avoid trouble?

TOM decides to add some *What fors* to his feedback about the broken ladder.

He has already suggested that someone might fall if something isn't done, and now he casually adds, 'I guess if someone falls in, you would have the job of rescuing them… and maybe a helicopter would have to be brought in. I wonder if you would be in trouble with your boss. And it would be terrible if other trekkers stopped coming to the park because it was dangerous… and if that happened, perhaps they wouldn't need a ranger… and I wonder if you could lose your job?'

Everyone agrees with TOM!

It quickly becomes obvious to the ranger that there just could be a bigger picture that he hasn't yet considered.

Now seemingly bursting with newfound enthusiasm, the ranger agrees that something needs to be done immediately to fix the loose rung and that he will get onto it straight away.

As TOM shakes the ranger's hand and sets off up the trail toward the peak, another thing becomes clear about feedback – it needs to be balanced if it is to be effective. Both the giver and the receiver need to be focussed on the same outcome and putting in the same amount of energy if they are to be successful. But often we find it difficult to see things the same as others do. It strikes him that the ranger probably had a detail focussed, (*Perfect* glasses on) view of the world at the moment he was talking with him. That's why he needed the extra *What fors* before he could make his decision to act. It would have been easy to think that the ranger was... lazy, or wrong... or even stupid, for not seeing things TOM's way. TOM is glad that he had remained calm and patient and had given the feedback in a way that the ranger needed to receive it, not just in the way that he needed to give it.

Enjoying the VISTA

The trail once again becomes steep as it leaves the glacier. The summer is on its way but at this altitude small pockets of snow

still lay behind rocks and in crevices hidden from the direct rays of the sun. TOM winds his way between and over huge boulders and along narrow ledges, but no matter which way the track leads him, the majestic walls of the peak are always visible high above his head. Every now and then he stops momentarily to gaze up at his objective – partly to check that he is on the right track, but more importantly, to assess his progress. He thinks of the times in his life when he has felt he hasn't been making any progress and remembers how that made him feel. Somehow the perception that he wasn't moving forward made him feel like he didn't want to move forward. And then there were times like now. Sure he is tired… and the track is steeper… and the air is thinner making breathing more difficult, but he can see that he is moving forward. It reminds him of similar times when even one tiny step forward gave him a boost. 'Maybe it's because we are built mainly to move forward,' he thinks. He has heard that the human body has many more muscles designed to make it move ahead than it has to make it go backwards. 'Maybe it is that simple. Maybe that's why getting ahead, making way, heading off, starting out… all have a positive feel, and giving up, turning back, feeling stuck, getting bogged down… all have a more negative feel.'

He glances briefly up at the mountain again and sets off with even more energy and commitment. 'Having a clear **Vision** is so important' he decides. 'And not just clear, it needs to be 'inspiring' as well. But inspiration is not much good without some sort of action being taken. I'm almost at the top of this mountain… and the Vision gave me the **Inspiration**… but what **Specific**ally did I have to do to get here? What did I have to pack, who did I have to tell what I was doing, what travel arrangements did I need to make, what maps did I need to buy, how much time did I need to allow… and thinking of time, how much do I have remaining to get up and down the mountain before dark?'

TOM checks his watch and estimates how much longer it will take him to reach the summit. He wonders if he would have come this far if he hadn't had some sort of time restriction. In his mind he has worked out where he needs to be at different parts of the journey. By doing this he actually has two ways of checking that he is making progress. He is pleased that he has encountered the PEA stand... the VISTA sign... the WIIFU... the Lemon Man... the MAL & BJ pub... the 'AAA' bridge... the Behavioural Blender... the Values Iceberg...the Pause Button, the Whadayawant Girl... the What 4 ladder... but being **Time-Bound** is spurring him on. It gives him cause for another pat on the back when he reaches these points at the times he expects.

He also realizes that it isn't only important that he will celebrate when he reaches the top, but also at each of these individual milestones along the way. At every **Assessable** point along the route he not only confirms that he is on course (sounds like more feedback!), but he also has the opportunity to celebrate his progress.

'When I look at my life,' he thinks, 'almost all of the times that I can remember being happy coincide with the times that I was moving forward or having even minor successes. They all meant something to me: When I learned to tie my own shoe laces, it meant I was growing up. Turning thirteen meant I was a 'teenager' and I was allowed to go some places on my own. Getting engaged, then married and having children meant that I was a fully-fledged adult and reaching milestones that my parents, peers and society had unconsciously placed on my path. Goalsetting and moving forward is an integral part of my life. It may not be the full Meaning of Life, but it certainly adds meaning to my life. I am a goal-achieving machine!'

He smiles to himself as he thinks... 'When I do good, I feel good... and when I feel good from doing good, I want to do even better! How cool is that?!'

Another glance upward confirms to him that the summit is actually getting closer (sometimes it feels like it isn't), and again his mind wanders and settles on a question that needs answering. '*What for*? What's in it for me?' (the WIIFM?) So often while growing up TOM has been warned about the dangers of becoming selfish – only considering his own needs at the exclusion of the needs of others. But as he considers this, he realises that, doing things for others (considering the WIIFU – What's In It For Us) has a WIIFM already built in. We usually do things for others because it makes us and them *feel* good. And actually... all motivation for doing things, for yourself or others, is catalysed by how it will make *you* feel. You eat because it will make you feel satisfied, you cry because it will provide you with a feeling of relief and release, you drink because you feel thirsty, you shout to express your feelings of excitement or anger... and you move toward your inspirational vision because you believe you will feel content when you turn it into reality.

At the exact time he had predicted, TOM hauls himself up the last boulder and steps onto the topmost peak of the mountain. Stretched out before him is yet another peak... and another... and yet another... on and on into the distance. He is exhausted, but at the same time ecstatic. He wonders if all the other peaks before him represent all the goals he still has in life. 'Perhaps it is important to have a string of goals to look forward to, otherwise... where would I go now? My first short-term goals: take some pictures, have a drink and a rest... and then... get safely down the mountain, which again is Time-Bound – before dark! '

Everyone agrees with TOM!

As he sits quietly taking in the magnificent view TOM chuckles to himself at the thought that the letters of his name spell out the core principles of how we achieve anything in our lives.

- ✓ He thinks about old Patsy and the tiny PEA in the palm of her hand as she talked about **Trust**.
- ✓ He marvels at how his VISTA **Objectives** guided him from his visualised success to the reality of standing proudly at the summit and assessing his achievement.
- ✓ And he counts the many WIIFM and WIIFU **Motivating** factors that kept him excited and enthusiastic and moving forward.

He also thinks about how he trusted in his ability... and the new boots that Ralph will have to buy him were a small motivating factor... but maybe the Objective plays a bigger role than he had first thought. Maybe the levels of Trust, Objectives and Motivation balance each other out. If the Trust is really solid, perhaps the Objective need not be as clear or the Motivation might not need to be as strong. And maybe if the Objective is powerfully inspirational – it's something that fires the imagination and gets the heart racing – then perhaps that's enough motivation in itself.

TOM is happy with his achievement and as he slowly threads his way down the mountain trail, he starts to consider how Trust, Objectives and Motivation can help him get the many other things he dreams about achieving in his life.

...and back in his day to day life?
TOM knows that he has learned a lot on his trip up the mountain, but as there is so much, he wonders if he has the ability to remember it all. 'Maybe if I reduce it down to just a set

of key **words**, that produce key **pictures** that trigger strong **feelings,** then the **action** might be that I remember it all!!'

He re-creates the story with the 12 models in 4 groups (and tacks VISTA on the end again):

TOM ate a *PEA*, saw the distant *VISTA* objective and imagined he saw the legendary *WIIFU*.

He ate *Lemons* and heard *MAL* give *BJ* some feedback.

He fixed the *Triple 'A'* bridge, used the *Behavioural Blender* and saw the *Values* Iceberg.

Then he *Paused* with the *Whadayawant* girl and crossed the *What 4 Feedback* ladder to view the *VISTA*.

Everyone agrees with TOM!

TOM meets BJ

A couple of years later, TOM is on a coffee break and nips out to the small café in the side street near his office. Sitting at a table in the corner is someone he thinks he recognizes. He is about the same age as TOM, dressed similarly like he has just left his own office, but the look on his face suggests that this man is deeply troubled about something. As TOM is looking across at him and trying to figure out where he knows him from, the man casually raises his gaze. Now he can see straight in his eyes, TOM recognizes him instantly. In a split second TOM is transported back to the scene where he first saw him – the bar, the man with the big nose, MAL – and all the events of that episode in the pub. BJ smiles a sort of 'sit with me if you want to but I'm not very good company' smile, and TOM decides it is worth a risk. He pays for his coffee and at BJ's request sits down at his table.

They exchange the usual pleasantries and recount the story of the day in the pub, but then the conversation takes an unexpected detour. BJ wants to talk and needs an ear. He can't figure out where he is going wrong in his life. Nothing seems to work out for him – he isn't getting anywhere in his job, he is bored and dissatisfied with his personal life and it seems like MAL is still the only friend he has. What he couldn't have known is that he has chosen to talk to the perfect person at this moment. After learning so much on his trip up the mountain, TOM decided to become a Life Coach. He has set up a small office upstairs in the main street and has built up quite a client list. It seems that everyone wants a piece of what TOM has – happiness, success, good relationships and a feeling of peace with himself and in his life.

As TOM tells BJ the story of the mountain and the lessons he has learned, BJ decides that this could be the opportunity he has been waiting for. 'This is it', he thinks. 'It's time to make a change!'

And indeed it is. TOM's next client has just postponed and BJ's next appointment isn't for another two hours… 'Let's do it!' BJ says, and the two head for TOM's office to make a start on BJ's new life.

BJ's Typical Day

TOM often started his coaching sessions with the question he now poses BJ.

'So... what does a typical day look like for you. From the time you get up until you go to bed again, let's talk about and write down everything that happens. But... here's the real challenge. I want you to think of your day as a list of agreements. Describe to me everything you do. Describe it in terms of it being an agreement with yourself or another person or with society or perhaps even with the law - and we will write it down, whether you got agreement or not. You see, I believe that TOM and triple 'A' can help you solve all of the issues that are hindering you from getting what you want in life.' BJ looked confused.

'Let's get started and you'll see what I mean - maybe there is a lesson here already. A famous philosopher named Johann Wolfgang von Goethe once said:

> 'Whatever you can do, or dream you can, begin it.
> Boldness has genius, power, and magic in it.'

Sometimes just making the first step, even if our heart is not completely in it, is enough to give the momentum to move forward. And sometimes we feel we don't have a clear enough picture of where we are going to make that step, but the movement can often trigger the clarity we were waiting for. But we'll talk more about visions and pictures later.'

And so they set to work…

BJ explains his agreements (mostly how he breaks them) and TOM takes some notes and also jots down the main ideas or models that could help BJ. It seems that BJ, like most of us riding on the merry-go-round of life, has some very challenging days to contend with. Here's what he writes:

1. *Agreement with self to get up on time linked to agreement with company to be at work on time.*
   On this particular day the stupid alarm clock doesn't go off again, so I'm a bit annoyed, but not surprised. It means that I'm probably going to be late for work again. Batteries just aren't as good as they used to be. Everyone knows I'm always late anyway. They should get used to it. I can't change the way I am.

   TOM's notes: I guess you could say that, as far as self-trust goes, BJ's account is well overdrawn. If his objective is to be on time, then he's off to a bad start. Somehow he just can't seem to get motivated to get his act together. But then again, he is amazingly successful at one thing – blaming something or someone else for his lateness. The fact that he chose to ignore the red light that told him the battery needed replacing seems to have been overlooked. - MAL and BJ

2. *Agreement with my wife to get milk and bread on the way home.*
   'BJ, wait a second.' 'What honey?!' I say, usually with a hint of anxiety and irritation. 'Quick, I'm running late!'

'Can you pick up some bread and milk on your way home tonight please?'

'Yeah, yeah, Ok. I'll try to remember, but I've got lots on today.' My wife is very methodical and always has detailed lists of things to do. I tend to not take things so seriously and don't like to be tied down by lists and detail. I just want to have fun.

TOM's notes: 'I'll try to remember.' Mmm... Interesting. I wonder how often he just tries to do things instead of just doing them. Sometimes we can put so much effort into trying to do something when we would be better off putting the effort into the doing. Maybe while we're focussing on how difficult something is going to be, we miss the opportunity to make it easy. – Responsibility + Behavioural Blends + Lemon Man

3.   *Agree with kids to take them to the pool after school.*
And then my wife calls out after me, 'And don't forget you promised to take the kids to the pool tonight.'
And I say, 'Ok, ok... I've gotta go.'

TOM's notes: How often do we say 'yes' when it really would be more appropriate to say 'no'? What would our life be like if we only committed to the things that we were reasonably sure we could accomplish? Instead we often tell people (and ourselves) what they want to hear. The upside of that is that we keep the peace for a moment. The downside is, every time we break a commitment, a tiny chunk of our self-esteem disappears. Self-esteem and self-trust are very closely linked. If I tell myself I'm going to do something, and then I do it, I feel good. When I feel good, my self-esteem goes up. When I do something and I feel good and my self esteem goes up, I'm more likely to trust myself enough to commit to the next thing, get it done, feel good... etc. Of course the reverse of this scenario is also true. I.e. If I don't do it... – TOM + Triple 'A'

4.   *Agreement to pick up friend and drive him to the station.*
When I get to my friend MAL's house, he has decided not to wait and has taken a taxi to the station. I mutter something like, 'Oh that's ridiculous! I was only ten minutes late! He should have waited. He knows I'm always late.' By the time I get to the station, MAL has already left on their usual train, and I feel angry and disappointed. I guess I also feel a bit guilty too, but then just shrug it off with something like, 'Oh well, it doesn't matter. MAL won't mind.' Inside I am beating myself up for what happened, but I probably won't tell MAL that.

TOM's notes: If he keeps breaking agreements with MAL, why should MAL trust him? Trust is made up of three major components: Persona (if BJ looks and sounds like someone that can be trusted) Effectiveness (if he does things that indicate that he is worthy of being trusted) Acceptance (if he accepts someone for the way they are and how they do things), they will probably trust him. BJ needs to see how he breaks trust. – TOM + PEA

5.   *Agreement with rail company to be polite to rail staff.*
I check my wallet for my ticket and realise it has expired, so I join the long queue to renew it. By the time I get to the window I have missed another two trains and I am frantic. 'Are you guys on a go-slow campaign?' I snap at the woman behind the ticket window. At this she decides to close her window telling me the ticket I want is available from the

auTOMatic vending machine. After finally negotiating the second queue and reaching the machine, I of course discover that I have no change in my pocket and the note acceptor is not working.

TOM's notes: Instead of taking action he tends to wait for actions to affect him. He seems to find it difficult to see the chains of events that lead to things happening to him. It's like a domino rally – one thing falls over which causes the next thing to fall over... until he finally stands back and says 'How did all that happen? It was nothing to do with me! – TOM + Response - ability + PAUSE

6. *Agreement with rail company to buy a ticket before boarding the train.*

Another train pulls in to the station so I make a dash for it and jump through the door as it is closing, just in time to be confronted by a ticket inspector who fines me £20 for not carrying a ticket. I'm always unlucky like that.

TOM's notes: Because of the string of events that have made him late, he is now rushing and taking risks. Now it is even more likely that something else will go wrong. By jumping through the door he is in danger of injuring himself or worse. And as for the ticket inspector... BJ hasn't worked out that the law is just another set of agreements. While we choose to live inside a community, we have a responsibility to conform to these laws... or change the laws... or move out of the community. Ignoring them will not make them go away. – TOM + Response-ability.

Everyone agrees with TOM!

7. Agreement with boss to complete a major project.
I finally get to my desk around 9.30 and I am greeted by a note asking me to go to the manager's office to report on my progress on an agreed project. The deadline was yesterday and I haven't finished it. My manager informs me that now I won't reach the target for my monthly bonus.

TOM's notes: If he takes on commitments he will need to follow them through. He seems to agree to do things without giving much thought to the logical consequences of getting or not getting it done. – VISTA + Response-Ability

8. Agreement with colleague to complete a document for her.
Around 10.30 I return to my desk to find my friend Mary with steam coming out her ears but not wanting to confront me with a problem – I was supposed to have completed a detailed document for her. It's strange, because she very rarely gets annoyed. I had told her yesterday that it was finished. She tells me that if I had warned her she would have come in early and finished it for me – she's so caring like that. She likes to keep the peace in the office so she tells me she will finish it and ring the cusTOMer to explain what happened. Lucky escape for me.

TOM's notes: BJ has completely ignored the fact that this colleague seems to have a different way to him of prioritising her values. She likes order, peace, reliability, routine – all things that seem to be low on BJ's list. He also doesn't seem to realise that lying damages his self esteem because it clashes with his own values – B. Blends + Values

9. *Agreement with team to email them with the report from the monthly managers meeting before their own team meeting later today.*

It is now 11.30am. 10am was the deadline we had set aside for emailing my team with news from yesterday's monthly managers meeting – they are all eager to see how they are faring, as a team and as individuals. I now have four angry emails in my inbox.

TOM's notes: The team's trust in BJ is diminishing every time he let's them down like this. They each have their own reasons for wanting to see the report as they have different sets of values and different Behavioural Blends. They all need to know the WIIFU. – BB's + Values + WIIFU

10. *Agreement with cusTOMer to buy a batch of old stock.*

I meet with the cusTOMer and tell her that it will be great if she buys the stock as it would help with my monthly figures and make space in the company storeroom. I don't know her very well but she seems very friendly. I was in a hurry but I still gave her all the details about the product and told her what it did and especially how much money she could make if she bought them. She just didn't seem to see that it would be a good opportunity for her to pick up a bargain.

TOM's notes: He has misread her B.B. completely and therefore has lessened the trust she has in him. He only talked about what he and his company would get out of the sale. He satisfied his objectives but never even asked her for hers! He discussed a 'What's In It For Us', but not the US that included the cusTOMer. – B.B.'s + WIIFU + TOM.

11. *Agreement with my team to present the objectives for the next three months.*

This is a meeting where I am meant to inspire my team with my vision for the next quarter. There are four (plus me) in this meeting and none of them seems to have understood my picture of where we are headed and the objectives I'm trying to set. Number one complains that I waffle too much and reckons that he has better ideas than me or the others. Number two asks a lot of questions and picks me up (and everyone else as well) on every detail. Three tells jokes, is irritated because everyone is ignoring him and so goes to sleep on the table. The last one sits quietly, doesn't contribute anything and seems to be bullied by number one, bored by number two and embarrassed by number three. It is a disaster!

TOM's notes: BJ seems to have an ideal team here because each Behavioural Style is represented, but he fails to communicate with each of them in the language of their particular style. The objectives may be inspirational and clear to him, but certainly not to the others. – B.B.'s + VISTA

12. *Agreement with road worker to give me the right directions.*
The road is blocked as I drive home and I find myself in an unfamiliar part of town. I pull over and get directions from a guy working on a jackhammer who tells me not to go left at the school or take the lane next to the hardware store or between the newsagent and the butchers and that the best way... Well I can't remember the best way because my head is full of what <u>not</u> to do. I get hopelessly lost and I am now even later than before. I get really frustrated with him and he promptly 'tells me where to go.' (and not too politely!)

TOM's notes: The road worker focussed on where BJ shouldn't turn, but BJ could have helped himself by asking a few What 4 questions, like... What road is the best to take? What road should I take next? What now? (Is it the best time to take that route?) And What for? (Why is this way better than any other?) – Whadayawant + PAUSE + What 4

13. *Agreement with police to drive my car in a way that abides by the traffic laws.*
Well, because I am running so late now I forget to keep an eye on my speed and don't see the radar trap on the side of the road. A week later I get a fine in the post and have to pay £60.

TOM's notes: Simple one. Just like the ticket inspector incident. The law is an agreement and a formal expression of our society's values. Disobeying the law is like acting contrary to one of those values. And like the old saying – 'If you do the crime you'll have to do the time', or in this case, 'Pay the fine!' – Response-Ability + TOM + Triple 'A' + Values

14. *Agreement with wife to be home on time.*
I finally stagger through the door about two hours late and my wife has left my dinner on the table to get cold. She just doesn't understand what an unlucky day I've had. She has left a note on the table that says, quite unfairly I think, 'Have gone to buy bread and milk, pick up the kids, and take them to the movie you promised to take me too!' Reading between the lines, I think she was angry. When they all get home later that night I discover that the kids aren't talking to me

because they had to walk three miles after swimming practice before their mother finished work and got there to pick them up.

TOM's notes: Having at least some understanding of how our relationship partners view the world is imperative if we are to live happy, balanced lives. It often takes some effort to attempt to see the world from another person's perspective, but the rewards will far outstrip the investment of time and energy. We like and trust people who see and do things in a way that seems familiar and comfortable to us. When you break trust by breaking an agreement, you reduce the chance of successfully working with this person to get anything done. They will also distrust your objectives and your motivation. - B.B.'s + Triple A

15. Agreement with Department of Internal Revenue to pay taxes.
On the end of the kitchen table is an official looking letter with my name on it. It seems I have forgotten to pay my tax and I've now been fined. It's been an expensive day – the rail inspector, the speeding fine and now this. I screw up the letter and throw it angrily at the window. It hits the glass, falls onto the windowsill, knocks over one of my wife's favourite vases which falls into the sink and smashes. I think someone is out to get me!

TOM's notes: Looks like I'll have to tell him his own MAL and BJ story again. He just doesn't seem to get it that his life and his actions are his responsibility. He would be able to respond in many different and more effective ways than this if he only chose to PAUSE and think about it. - MAL and BJ + PAUSE

16. Agreement with myself and others to reward successes.
On the other end of the table I completely miss another plain looking envelope with my name on it. Reluctantly I slit it open, prepare for the worst and begin to read. I entered a writing competition a couple of weeks ago and the letter is to tell me I have won third prize. 'Great' I say to myself, sarcastically. 'Can't even win first prize! What a loser. That just matches the rest of my day.'

TOM's notes: There he goes again, missing an opportunity to learn. It is vitally important that we first of all give ourselves every chance to succeed by expecting it (talking about what we want). But it is even more important to reward ourselves when we do succeed or even partially succeed (Keep our agreements). Every acknowledgement of a step forward (Assessing and self-Feedback) gives us a dose of chemical 'upper' (builds self – trust) that propels us on toward our vision. This is our personal WIIFU: the carrot, the pot of gold, the Feel Good Factor. – TOM + VISTA + Triple 'A' + 3 E's + What 4 + Whadayawant.

17. *Agreement with myself to lower my golf handicap and learn to play the piano.*
   I think I could be a much better golfer except for all the bad luck I have. Other players always seem to beat me. Or often it's the weather that causes me to play so badly. And I have piano lessons every week. I've always wanted to play the piano. I'm so busy though I don't have time to practice.

TOM's notes: We all have a certain amount of natural ability in whatever we choose to do, but even someone with a large amount of personal skill has to set goals and then practice. We all have to work at building our self-belief, self-confidence or self-trust as we also develop our skills and become more effective at something. His conversations are laced with statements about problems instead of solutions; about how he is no good at this and can't do that and how he hasn't got any money for lessons and...and... – TOM+ PEA + VISTA + WIIFU.

18. Agreement with kids to communicate with them in a reasonable manner.
I yell at the kids to tidy up their rooms before they go to bed, but they never listen. It's always the same argument. 'Your room is a mess!' 'So what?' they say, 'It's my room!' 'Tidy it up!' I reply to them, and they say, 'Why should I – your room's untidy Dad!' And I say, 'Never mind my room. Just do it because I say so!' They don't have any respect for me at all.

TOM's notes: Most of the things his children have learned, they have learned from him. And even half their genes came from him. Life would be much easier if he looked at the way in which he likes other people to communicate with him. BJ doesn't like being yelled at, so why would his children? He described what he didn't want and then expected them to do what he did want. Not very logical. His feedback style was unstructured and aggressive. TOM + PAUSE + What 4 + Values.

19. Agreement with self to pass my business school exams.
I go to college a couple of times a month. I can't always make it because there's often a good football match on that night and a man's got to have his social life. Besides, the course is really stupid and most of the stuff I'll never use. It's strange though, the stuff I hate is always the stuff they put in the exams!

TOM's notes: If he wants that particular qualification then he needs to do that course – not a course that is re-designed just for him. Often we stand too close to the fire and then wonder why we get burned. It is a 'cause and effect universe' – if you want this, then you will need to do that. Simple. Don't argue and complain about it. Use that energy to just get it done.

20. Agreement with self to go to bed early so I can wake up easier in the morning.
I always fall asleep in front of the television, usually thinking about what a lousy day I've had and hoping that TOMorrow will be better.'

TOM's notes: Agreements with self are often called 'self-discipline'. BJ has talked himself into this pattern by saying things like 'I always...' or 'I usually'. By talking about it he keeps remembering and picturing it. This then subconsciously becomes his vision and his body reacts to this vision by doing what he expected it would – going to sleep. By adapting this vision and expecting a different result (picturing himself going to bed early) the event will change (he will go to bed early) and his evaluation in the morning will be that he 'can' go to bed early, which will change his expectation for the next night. – 3 E's + MAL

Everyone agrees with TOM!

TOM's Summary notes: After assessing every one of these agreements it is obvious that BJ will have to adapt his thoughts and behaviours so as to get different results and then be able to give himself favourable assessments. Each of these twenty agreements is an example of TOM and the Triple 'A' Model in action.

Over the next few months TOM helps BJ's work through his day and assists him to see that there is one central theme to all his woes – broken agreements. He shows him all the models and coaches him on how to apply what he learns to each of the issues that seem to ruin his day.

5

TOM Coaches BJ

TOM coaches BJ on how to build relationships and get things done – is there anything else that's important? Following are all the coaching sessions that TOM had with BJ, so let's eavesdrop and find out what BJ learned. Remember, this is TOM talking to BJ, not the author talking to you, the reader. TOM began...

Choice

When asked a question about the different chances he had taken in his life, I once heard Roger Daltrey say:

'Life is like a railway station. You can either stand on the platform or you can catch the trains.'

I'd like to add a macabre and perhaps challenging extension to this thought:

'You can either stand on the platform... or you can jump in front of the train!'

Each and every moment of each and every day, you can either choose to live or choose to die. If you choose to live then you will need to accept all the logical consequences associated with that decision. These include a whole raft of ideas / opportunities / challenges, from keeping your body healthy to finding love and affection to providing food, shelter and security for yourself and others – those for whom you accept at least some responsibility.

Everyone agrees with TOM!

And speaking of others, there are more than six and a half billion of them on this little planet. Regular communication with at least some of them is inescapable. Wouldn't it be great if <u>every</u> time we spoke to someone, our message was received just the way we intended it to be? And better still… wouldn't it be great if the receiver of the message actually agreed with us AND did what we suggested?

And what about the reverse? How much easier would our lives be if we always received the message (and the real meaning) and felt compelled to agree and then act on it?

Agreements

Every aspect of our lives is connected to some sort of *agreement*. It's when we start exchanging information about that agreement, we come unstuck. And often it's the simplest agreements that cause us the most trouble.

If you agree to meet me at the pub at 8 o'clock, but don't arrive until 10 o'clock, there are a few questions that need to be asked about the communication between us.

1. What were our expectations? Did I trust your commitment to be there at 8 o'clock? And based on all the other times in your life when you've been late, did you trust yourself to be there on time?
2. Was it absolutely clear what both of us expected of ourselves and of each other? Were we both clear, not only on what time to turn up, but what the objectives were for the night? What did we want to achieve by meeting up?
3. Why were you motivated to do something other than keep your agreement? What motivating factor would have motivated you to be on time?

All strong and effective agreements are founded on three criteria:

Trust – trust on both sides leads to clear, honest and committed agreements
Objectives – both parties need to know exactly what is required
Motivation – there has to be something to be gained by both parties

Every aspect of our lives involves getting things done. Even if you agree to do nothing, it takes some thought or effort to organise it. It makes good sense to have a way of making this process enjoyable and effective. This is where the TOM model can make it easy for us. TOM always gets things done because he gets strong agreements. How?

He builds **trust** and sets clear **objectives** that are both meaningful and **motivating** to himself and any others involved.

And if you stop and think about it... (Go on, do it now!) ...everything you want to do starts with an agreement with yourself. Of course, self-agreements are also based on TOM.

Self-Trust
Let's say I feel like I need a holiday. I don't know about you, but there always seems to be a period of time where I engage in a mental argument with myself about why I think I need or deserve a holiday. How do I justify to myself that I have earned this holiday or that it should be me who goes rather than someone else in my office. Only one person can go at this particular time, so why is it my turn? Or how do I justify it to my wife or partner that I want to go to my favourite destination, not theirs? And then there's the cost – can I afford it? I could spend it

on getting new carpet for the apartment, so how can I channel funds into something as frivolous as a pleasure jaunt? Maybe I could half turn it into a business trip and do some networking while I'm away. Or maybe I just *have to* go because my mother / aunt / cousin isn't getting any younger and I don't know...'

If I completely trusted my judgement, would there be all this concern? If I truly believed that I always made the best decision in the circumstances, wouldn't I just go ahead and do it?

So now..., let's imagine I have exhausted all the mind blah-blah and I have at least a tenuous agreement with myself that I deserve a holiday. Maybe TOM can help me organise it? He certainly helped me make my decision – I finally trusted myself to at least commit to setting the objectives and start organising the holiday.

So now the next question: 'Do I trust myself to organise it?'

As I rummage through the chaotic filing system of my brain for similar past experiences, how many instances do I find of times when I have promised myself a vacation and ... I didn't actually get around to making a booking? When I announce my tentative plans to mates and family, do they roll about laughing and scoffing loudly that they've heard it all before? And now my self-esteem monitor chimes in and throws up the thousands of other times when I have... promised to write a letter but haven't, promised to keep a secret but didn't, promised to be home on time but wasn't...

If my self-esteem (and inherent self-trust) was depicted as a block of ice, these seemingly inconsequential broken promises would be all the tiny cracks, chips and fissures that weaken my resolve and dissolve any self-trust I may have accumulated through the promises I have kept. These same flaws are the ones that give rise to the tiny voice that whispers to us just milliseconds after we speak up about any new commitment. It often sounds something like:

'You're late!' and 'But you promised!' and 'Why didn't you call me?' ... ... 'I knew I'd fail.' ... and 'No way you're going to make it by then!' ...'You must be joking!'

So what can you do to build self-trust? Easy. Remind yourself of all the times that you did keep your agreements and commitments. Every time you keep one from now on – celebrate. Write it down and remember it often. You will gradually start reprogramming your self-beliefs to a point where they will back you up when you make a big commitment instead of criticising you.

Personal Objectives

Am I really clear on the objectives of the holiday? Is it to help me relax or is it to create an adventure that excites me? Is it to see relatives or to go shopping? Is it to fulfil a lifelong dream or is it just on a whim because I suddenly felt like it? And after I have answered these questions, then I need to set VISTA objectives (I can show you how to do that when we start building your personal toolkit for getting things done and still having a good time).

Personal Motivation

As human beings, one of our principal motivators is to 'feel' successful or to be part of something that is successful. To make sure my holiday actually happens, how will I choose WIIFU factors for myself that catapult me into action? What are the things that excite me into taking risks? What are the factors that make me want to move, take action, begin, start… and get past all the initial barriers or fears or apathy that prevents me from taking that first step and seeing it through to the end?

In TOM's Toolkit we will of course work with the TOM model as well as all the concepts and ideas from the trip to the mountain. As you will see, they all play an important part in bringing TOM to life and ensuring we achieve the many goals we either have chosen, or have been given to us, in our lives.

TOM's Tool Kit

The TOM model

Absolutely anything you want in life you can get with TOM. Whether it is an agreement with yourself or another person, group, company, team or organisation, the process is exactly the same. No matter who you are or what you do – single or partnered, businessperson or sportsperson, team manager or team member, buyer or seller, leader or follower – you can get the most out of every life situation and every relationship by using one simple set of guidelines. TOM.

Trust – Build it on both sides to get clear, honest, committed agreements.

Objectives – Set them so that both parties have a vivid picture of what the final outcome looks and feels like and how you intend to get there by working together.

Motivation – Ensure that there is enough on both sides – we only ever do things that give us some type of reward or help us to avoid something we don't want.

Trust with PEA
Relationships, whether personal or business, are built on TRUST
that comes from 3 main sources:
- *Persona*

Based on a person's appearance and behaviour,
we begin to decide whether or not this is a
person we can possibly trust.
- *Effectiveness*

If this person matches our original
perception of their personality, i.e. they are good at a particular
task or they are good at relating, then we start to trust them a
little more.
- *Acceptance*

If they are sensitive to our needs and not critical of our
personality or behaviour, then our level of trust in them
continues to rise. If any of these aspects of trust are ignored,
trust in a relationship will begin to decline. In short:

> *'If they look like they can do it, they are doing it and they
> don't judge me for the way I do it, then I will probably trust them.'*

And REMEMBER… Ground Rules Rule!
Every successful relationship or effective interaction is based on
a set of ground rules. We all have our set of ground rules –
things that we think we should do and things we think others
should do. Knowing what they are can help you build trust in
yourself and with others. Breaking ground rules can cause
excitement, but generally brings confusion and a loss of trust – in
the process, self and others.

Do: smile, be friendly, be punctual, be reliable, be honest, be
open…
Don't: frown, be aggressive, turn up late, let people down, lie, be
closed…

And if someone doesn't trust you, take responsibility. Have you broken their ground rules?

Objectives with VISTA

Visualised, Inspiring, Specific, Time-bound, Assessable objectives are more powerful and easier to achieve. If every time you want to do something, no matter how big or small it is, you consider these five points, you will have a  vastly improved chance of achieving your goal. And the most powerful and therefore most important is, **Visualised**. A clear picture of where you are going or what the final outcome will look and feel like is vital in every single task we attempt to achieve. Everything else in your VISTA plan hinges on this vision.

Everything you have created for yourself up until now, good and bad, you have arrived at via the exact same process. Think about it. It all started with a mental image.

Everyone agrees with TOM!

Visualised Objectives – What is the mental picture you have of success? What does it look, sound, feel, smell and taste like? In this imaginary scene, who is there, what is happening and, this is vital – how does it **feel** emotionally?

Inspirational Objectives – This aspect is a result of the scene you have visualised. Is it powerful enough to move you into action?

Specific Objectives – What exactly are the specific steps or stages you need to pass through before you match your vision. There may be just one major picture of success you have in mind, or several smaller achievements that combined will give you your all important 'feel good factor'.

Time-bound Objectives – Place deadlines on each specific step, as well as the final outcome. Goals are most effective when they are just far enough out of reach to give an eventual sense of accomplishment, but not so far as to demotivate.

Assessable Objectives – It is imperative that there be points at regular intervals where your progress is noticeable. Knowing where these points are, imagining how it will feel when you get there, acknowledging and celebrating their achievement, are all vital steps on the road to success.

Motivation with WIIFU

Scientists and psychologists pretty much agree that what moves us forward is the future vision of how we are going to FEEL after  we do or we don't do something. Be it human, animal or vegetable, we are all motivated by the same thing – we move towards what we want and away from things we don't want.

Plants grow toward the sun, their roots grow toward water. Animals chase food, search for shade and run from danger. As humans, we think things like: 'I'll cook this, so I can taste that.' Or... 'I'll talk to you because it makes me happy.' 'I'll avoid her so I don't have to feel uncomfortable'... 'I'd better do that, otherwise I'll feel guilty'... and even... 'I'll help them so they can feel safe and that will make me feel good.' You see, even when we do things for others, we do it because of how we believe we will feel afterwards – good for helping or bad for not helping. Either or both beliefs about the future will propel us into action. And by some weird law of logic, even what we don't want turns out to be something we want. Huh?? I'll explain. If a big dog is chasing me, it may look like I am running *away* from it, but I am actually running *towards* something. Safety. Make sense?

The botTOM line is ultimately, What's In It For ME, but considering What's In It For <u>Us</u> is probably healthier and again, *feels* better. And whether it's for self or others, it's a bonus for us. I do love doing things for others; my kids, my wife, my friends – and sometimes complete strangers* – but I also know I get a great feeling from doing that.

(* Take a look at the Join-me.co.uk website for more on this☺)

Everyone agrees with TOM!

And did you know, your job is to motivate your boss, not just the people who work for you? 'How and to do what?' you ask:

You motivate them to help you, be pleasant to you, to promote you, to give you important tasks, to give you time off, to approve holidays when you want them, to support your decisions, to give you a pay rise. Find out what motivates them and provide it for them! If they like punctuality, be punctual. If they want a pay rise, show them that assisting you with your goals will assist them with theirs. Put simply: show them how to get what they want by helping you get what you want. A real WIIFU!

So... how do you use TOM?

Use it as a checklist before you ask yourself or anyone else to do something. Just ask:

1. Do I trust myself/him/her to do this task? If not, how can I go about building *Trust* – of me by them and by them of me? (see PEA)
2. Are the Objectives clear and sufficiently compelling to get me/them to commit to the task?
3. Are there sufficient and appropriate Motivating factors that will motivate me/them to do the task?

Note: Nothing will happen unless there is an opportunity to gain some type of reward or avoid some type of forfeit. And sometimes avoiding a forfeit may be the only reward we get, but if it makes us feel good or brings us relief, we'll probably choose to take on the task.

So… how do you use PEA to build Trust?
If you want others to trust you, consider these questions:

Persona: Do you look, sound or seem like someone who can be trusted?
Effectiveness: Are you effective at getting things done, achieving results, being a friend?
Acceptance: Do you accept others for the way they appear and what they do? Do you accept them as people and encourage them to adapt their behaviour?

So… how do you use VISTA to set objectives?
V – Visualise and see it vividly. E.g. If you're thirsty, picture your favourite drink.
I – Check that it inspires you not action. Does the image of this drink make your mouth water?
S – Add specific details. How exactly will you go about getting your drink? Ring a friend, take some money, meet at the pub…
T – is it time-bound? Set time limits on each step as well as the final objective. Call friend at 5pm, bank at 6, pub at 6.30…
A – Assess and apply rewards to each specific step and each time-bound stage. Ring friend… tick, go to bank… tick, arrive at pub on time… tick… etc.

So… how do you use a WIIFU to establish Motivation?
1. Find your own Feel Good Factors and you now have a stack of rewards to motivate yourself to move forward.
2. Find another person's Feel Good Factors and you have found ways to motivate them too.

Note: Both of these options above are related to *Values*, which I mentioned in *TOM and the Mountain*, but will also be covered a little later in the book.

The Lemon Man
…and the Balance between Performance and Well-being

The words we use create pictures that create feelings that produce behaviour. The only reason we 'feel' or 'do' anything is as a direct result of a chemical change in our bodies. If you want to feel different, then change the images in your mind. You are really just a bag of chemicals driven by an electrochemical brain. Sorry about that ☹. I know I'm oversimplifying things, but it is basically true. You may have spirit, soul, dreams and all sorts of other things going on, but at a basic 'thought – belief – action' level, you create what you picture in your mind.

You have something in your brain called an RAS (Reticular Activating System) and it's a part of your brain's hardware that is responsible for focusing your attention. Of all the millions of pieces of information in our environment, we need to focus on only one piece at a time if we want to achieve success at almost any task. Our RAS works continuously to assist us with this process. If you focus on something, you get a mental picture of it, it stimulates your body to make you feel something and that feeling makes you do things. So what's the message? Be careful what you focus on!

Every thought you have, every picture your mind creates, produces a physical reaction in your body. Isn't that an amazing (and possibly scary) thought? – especially when you think of some of the things you think, see and imagine. That's why whenever you think about any event in your life, the mental pictures trigger the exact same feelings and sensations that were produced in your body on the actual day it happened. That's why you shiver when you think of the time you cut your finger and laugh when you remember something funny – your brain thinks it just happened all over again and sends down the same chemicals.

A big part of this chemical process is involved with storing your memories. Your brain links together thoughts that have some sort of similarity or connection. It forms long strings of neurons based on the messages it receives from your senses. The more similar messages you give it, the stronger the memory. It's the basis of something called…

En-Lightning Learning

The theory of multiple intelligences was developed in 1983 by Dr. Howard Gardner, professor of education at Harvard University. It suggests that the traditional notion of intelligence, based on I.Q. testing, is far too limited and relates mainly to Logical intelligence. Dr. Gardner proposed that there are at least eight different intelligences or ways the brain acquires knowledge and remembers things. To these eight some people add another two that they say are not sufficiently highlighted under Dr Gardner's system – Emotion and Drama.

Everyone agrees with TOM!

These ten intelligences, first mentioned on page 13, are repeated here with a touch more detail:

Musical intelligence (**music**/rhythm smart)
    – links to hearing, sound, tone, pitch, rhythm
Intrapersonal intelligence (**self** smart)
    – links to personal reflection, thinking, deciding
Logical- intelligence (**logic**/reasoning smart)
    – links to order, flow and sequence
Drama Intelligence (**story** smart)
    – links to story telling, narrative, describing, legend

Kinesthetic intelligence (**sense** smart)
    – links to body, taste, smell, movement, touching
Emotional Intelligence (**feeling** smart)
    – links to happiness, sadness, excitement, guilt, fear
Linguistic intelligence (**word** smart)
    – links to words, significance, language, idiom
Visual intelligence (**picture** smart)
    – links to colour, shape, area, depth
Interpersonal intelligence **(people** smart)
    –   links to learning and comparing with others
Naturalist intelligence (**nature** awareness smart)
    – links to anything in the world of nature

And to make it even easier to remember theses ten intelligences, you can use a short story or sentence using the first letters. Like…

My Industrious Little Dog
Kicked Every Little Vampire In Naples.

So… to remember anything, and fast…

1. Identify **Key** Words from the detail and…
2. Link **Images** that trigger…
3. **Feelings** that create physical or imaginary…
4. **Actions** of a 'story' that involve all ten intelligences.
5. **Review**, Repeat (emphasising different intelligences),
6. Repeat ALL these steps several times

And the really short version…

If you hear something, then see it, then touch it and then tell someone else about it, you'll probably remember it.

Every one of these experiences creates another string of brain cells. Just the same as you need a lot of bricks to create an effective wall, you also need a lot of neurons to create a strong memory.

So… how do you use the lessons from The Lemon Man?
1. Use all your senses to help you remember something.
2. Be careful what you focus on.
3. Live a balanced life – focus on both Tasks and Feelings.

MAL and BJ

MAL could teach you a lot about personal responsibility. Knowing that we make, assist and let things happen will

eliminate blame and justification and help you to be response-able. That is, able to respond to any situation with an enlightened response rather than an auTOMatic reaction. Every one of us is at least partly responsible for the events of our lives and the perceptions others have of us. We either **Make** them happen, **Assist** them to happen or **Let** them persist.

Just like when you were punched in the bar the first time; did you **make** it happen? 'Yes.'
And the second time; did you **assist** it to happen? 'Yes.'
And when you could see trouble brewing, but didn't leave; did you **let** it happen? 'Yes.'

And the same is true for everything else that happens in our lives – we either:
Make things happen by actively *creating* the circumstances that brought about the event
Assist things to happen by *contributing* to the circumstances that brought about the event, or
Let them happen by *allowing* those circumstances to persist.

MAKE
ASSIST
LET
OR

BLAME
JUSTIFICATION

RESPONSE - ABILITY

If we aren't doing a MAL, then we are probably doing the opposite – blaming something or someone else or justifying why we need to do it or just making excuses. But in the end, most of us get to that 'Oh yeah!' moment when we realize that it probably is our responsibility. My life is my responsibility. Your life is your responsibility. If there are things I want, I need to work out how to get them. If there are things I don't want, I have to figure out how to stop or move away from them. And it's the same for all of us.

A bit harsh you think? Well what about this: We at least *let* whatever happens affect the way we think, then feel and then act. And who controls your thoughts? Not sure? Well… here's a test. Don't think about water… and especially don't think of a river … or a lake… or an ocean! How did you go? I'll bet that I at least influenced, if not controlled, your thoughts for a moment so that you couldn't help thinking about water! It's just about impossible to stop thoughts flooding in… (Oops, sorry about the water reference ☺).

But here's the real crux of the matter:

We may not be responsible for the thoughts that come into our heads, but we certainly are responsible for the ones we act on.

If you're not, who is? Who can you blame? Can you really justify your actions when you know that ultimately, only you have the power of choice over your emotions and behaviour? I always think it's funny to hear parents telling their kids to 'Stop misbehaving', 'Don't be rude', or…'Stop being so silly!' and even 'Stop sulking' or 'Don't be so angry!' I know I said these things to my children. What I was really saying was, 'Do as an immature child something that I find almost impossible to do as a mature adult.' I was also asking for an outcome that I didn't want. By saying 'Don't be rude!' the mental picture I was creating for them was one of being rude. Then they had to cross it out. Then they had to come up with their own picture of what I really wanted. It would have been much more effective to say what I did want. i.e. 'Be polite please.' I now know I do have the ability to respond as I choose to different situations and paint pictures of what I want to happen instead of the opposite. I do have Response-Ability – and so do you.

Everything that happens to us is either as a direct or an indirect result of a choice we have made. A big claim you say? Some examples might help.

If I am driving down the road and another car races through a stop sign and crashes into the side of me, how can that be as a result of a choice I have made? I chose to drive. If I hadn't chosen to drive I wouldn't have been behind the wheel when a car hit me. 'Ok' you say, 'what if I was a passenger?' Same deal. If I choose to be a passenger in a car on busy roads, then I take on all the inherent risks of that choice. It is unrealistic to think that there won't be accidents and just as unrealistic to think that it will never happen to me. I always have a choice.

More on Choices
Abraham Maslow's Hierarchy of Needs suggests that there are five levels of needs about which, if we choose to carry on with our human life, we will have to make choices and decisions. It seems as good a framework as any on which to continue a discussion on our personal responsibility to make choices.

The hierarchy is shown in reverse order on the following page starting with Basic Survival through to Self Actualisation.

Basic Survival needs – This is the 'food, shelter and procreation level'. If I choose to live then these at least are prerequisites.

Security – I can choose to make sure that something doesn't eat me, or worse still, trample on my feelings!

Affiliation – Let's face it, we're herd animals (well most of us). People like people who are like them. As I mentioned in The Enlightened Response, we all choose to be members of some sort of club or bunch of people who are like us. Even eccentrics have their eccentricity as a common theme.

Self Esteem – and now that I've found my friends to hang out with, I need to know that I bring something unique to the party. I can choose to find my niche and be proud of it, or choose to remain isolated and berate myself for it.

Self Actualisation – I can choose to recognise my part in the great game of life and in the universe and live to my full potential and become everything that I am capable of becoming.

At each level there are sets of accompanying choices. While we're here, there is no escaping our Response-Abilities!

And just as we create most of the events of our lives, or at least our responses to them, we equally have a part to play in the creation of other's perceptions of us – we make, assist or let them happen as well. The two criteria they have for assessing us are what we do and what we say. If we are more thoughtful about what we do and say, we actively assist the forming or their perceptions of us. It may be that you haven't really done anything wrong. But it could be that, whatever it was that you did, somehow it was interpreted by others differently than you intended. Either way, you can't escape the fact that what you did contributed to their perception.

Everyone agrees with TOM!

One of the ways we get to know other's perceptions of us, and they get to know our perceptions of them, is through **feedback**, which we'll talk about in more detail a little later.

So... how do you use MAL and BJ?
Whatever happens, ask yourself these questions and answer them honestly?

1. How did I **make** this happen?
2. How did I **assist** this to happen?
3. How did I **let** this happen? (including how I let it affect the way I feel)

Very quickly you will become aware of how you Make, Assist and Let everything happen in your life. But for now, the choice is yours. Are you going to think more like a new MAL or an old BJ?

Remember the 3 E's of Life
You can change your Expectations
You can change your Evaluations
And you can probably change at least half of the Events.

Take control of the 3 E's and control your life!

The Triple 'A' Bridge – Communication is about building bridges between people. Sometimes you need to build a bridge to get to someone but also make sure it reaches them where they are, not where you want them to be.

Sometimes you need to work together so you can cross together – Assess the bridge, Agree to work together and Adapt along the way if you need to.

The focal point of any communication is to get AGREEMENT, (Agreement on 'what happened, what's happening and what's going to happen') and getting agreement involves three main elements:

Trust – Trust on both sides leads to more honest and committed agreements. Make sure you have trust and you are more likely to agree to each other's...

Objectives – Both parties need to be clear on exactly what each wants to achieve from the agreement. Sometimes the objective is itself motivating. Sometimes you need more...

Motivation – There needs to be either some type of reward or an opportunity to avoid something we don't want – which is another type of reward. Always ensure that the logical consequence of achieving an objective is something you want to happen.

And the Triple 'A' part?

You need to **AGREE**:
1. on how you are going to work together (establish Trust)
2. on what your common goals are (set Objectives)
3. on what both the positive or negative logical consequences are of reaching or not reaching your objective (Motivation)

You need to **ADAPT**:
1. to each others needs so that you both get what you want (to maintain Trust)
2. to the needs of the task you are working on (to maintain clear Objectives)
3. the rewards so that the *feel good factor* is maintained (maintain Motivation)

You need to constantly **ASSESS**:
1. that you are still happy with the way you work together (assess level Trust)
2. progress on the goals you have set (stages of the Objectives)
3. that the rewards and or negative consequences (Motivating factors) have been applied.

And what about you and TOM?

TOM and Triple 'A' work just as well with yourself as they do with others. How? It's like imagining there are at least two different voices inside your head and you can negotiate with them using TOM.

AGREE:

Trust: Do you trust yourself to do it? (whatever *it* is) What's your track record like? What persona do you project? Are you effective at what you do? Do you accept yourself/others?

Objectives: Have you agreed with yourself exactly what your objectives are and how you are going to get there? Do the objectives excite you?

Motivation: Why are you doing it? What will be your reward for doing it or the logical consequences of not doing it? Are they enough to move you into action?

ADAPT:

Trust: Are you honest enough to adapt your behaviour so as to trust yourself more?

Objectives: Are you flexible enough to adapt and change your plan if you need to?

Motivation: Are you prepared to adapt your rewards to maintain momentum?

ASSESS:

Trust: Do you acknowledge all your successes so that you build trust in your ability?

Objectives: Are there assessable objectives en route by which to measure your progress? Is each of them an objective within itself that you can be proud of achieving?

Motivation: Do you apply the consequences at the assessable milestones as well as at the final objective? Most importantly – make sure you reward yourself for achieving!!

So... how do you use Triple 'A' Communication?

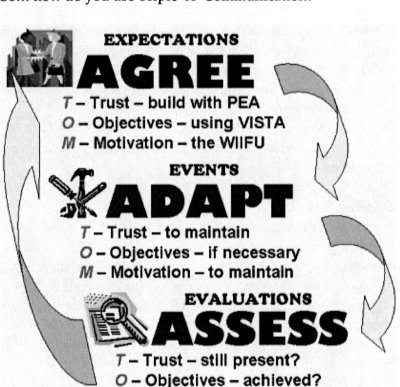

EXPECTATIONS

AGREE

T – Trust – build with PEA
O – Objectives – using VISTA
M – Motivation – the WIIFU

EVENTS

ADAPT

T – Trust – to maintain
O – Objectives – if necessary
M – Motivation – to maintain

EVALUATIONS

ASSESS

T – Trust – still present?
O – Objectives – achieved?
M – Motivation – apply rewards!

The Behavioural Blender

I don't know about you, but my personality, the way I feel and the way I see the world, seems to change from moment to

moment, day to day. Accurately assessing anyone's personality is an impossibility. The best we can aim for realistically is empathy – an understanding of what someone might be feeling and thinking based on our knowledge of how we, and they, might see things.

Be accepting of another person's behaviour. The wiring of our brains, and consequently our views of the world, were basically formed between the time we were conceived and the age of about ten. (3) *By the second decade of life, (brain) growth levels off and pruning begins.* (i.e. the number of brain connections actually *decreases* after age 10!) We are a product of our genes and the environment in which we spent our early years. Until we become aware of this, we often act purely out of habit. Be careful – it's easy to judge your own behaviours as good and others' as bad, and vice versa.

(4) By age 3, 80% of synaptic connections are already made. Increased experiences define the wiring of an infant's brain.

How much and for how long do these early life experiences impact on our lives?

Author's note: My cousin, Marion, at age 64 still remembers having to unpick her sewing at her new school because 'that's not the way we do it here'. She was aged seven at the time. At age 11 she decided to stop answering questions when she was whacked with 'the cane' for giving an incorrect response. These events shape our thinking for a lifetime.

We all use a blend of different behavioural styles to communicate and to get what we want. Although there are many ways of viewing the world, human behaviour tends to be a blend of several styles. It's a bit like carrying around these four different ways of doing things in a backpack and only bringing them out when we need to. If you can imagine they are like four different sets of eyeglasses that you put on when you want to see the world from someone else's viewpoint. If you put on two sets at once, you get a blend of those two viewpoints.

As individuals we are a unique mixture of these styles or habitual behaviours, with one or two styles dominating much of the time. There are numerous systems for categorising the various styles of human behaviour and the following four styles comprise one simple system for this purpose.

Behavioural Blends is a system for instantly assessing individuals by identifying a few key behaviours i.e. the simple and habitual things they do and say. It's like they have thrown only two of the four sets of eye glasses into the blender. What comes out is a pair that allows us to see things with the same blend of styles that they use.

As the poet Robert Burns once said:

"Oh wad some Power the giftie gie us,

to see oursels as others see us!"

Which roughly translates to:

'Wouldn't it be great if we could see what others see when they look at us?'

By understanding how your own particular view of the world has developed to be different from others', you can learn how to support and understand those with whom you live, play and work – colleagues, family, friends, bosses, cusTOMers...

Behavioural Styles

There are four styles that blend together to make up your Behavioural Blend

CONTROL – task focussed / outspoken

If you are seeing with your *Control* glasses on, you are probably outspoken and tend to *tell* people things; you like summaries, directness, the 'short' story, confrontation and strength. You probably also like doing the task and leading the team.

Main focus: "What do you want and when do you want it? Will I be in control of myself and others? My way is the best way."

PERFECT – task focussed / quieter

If you are seeing with your *Perfect* glasses on, you are probably quieter and *ask* more questions; like detail, accuracy, precision, cleanliness and correctness. You probably also like doing the task the right way and monitoring the quality of the team's results.

Main focus: "What quality of job do you want, why do you want it, what are the specifications, how accurate should it be, precisely what are the issues and is it the correct thing to do? My way is the right way."

ENTERTAIN – people focussed / outspoken

If you are seeing with your *Entertain* glasses on, you are probably outspoken and tend to *tell* people things; you like recognition, excitement, talking, change, colour and bright lights. You probably also like everyone to see you doing the task and you like entertaining the team.

Main focus: "Who is going to be there, will they recognise me, will it be fun and how can I make them like me? My way is the most enjoyable way and I will get credit for that."

MEDIATE – people focussed / quieter

If you are seeing with your *Mediate* glasses on you are probably quieter and *ask* more questions; you like stability, routine, teamwork, anonymity and peace. You probably also like everyone to be involved and sharing in doing the task, you like being part of the team and you strive to keep the peace within the team.

Main focus: "How can we all work together harmoniously, in an orderly fashion and create win/win for all those involved? My way is the easiest and most peaceful way for all involved."

IMPORTANT: No one style is better than another. We all have a bit of every style in us. Being a balanced individual means being able to blend behaviours from each style as the situation requires.

So… how do you use Behavioural Blends?

✓ Listen to the feedback you get from other people. How you appear to them is often vastly different to how you appear to yourself.

✓ Use all the feedback and information you have to help you better understand your own Behavioural Blend and the Behavioural Blends of those around you.

✓ Communicate with others the way they would like you to communicate with them. For example, if someone seems to be speaking from a *Control* style or perspective, make sure you give them three or four bullet points, be direct and to the point. Talk about detail and precision to someone wearing their *Perfect* eye glasses or about excitement and adventure to someone wearing *Entertain* glasses. If it appears that they could be wearing their *Mediate* perspective, keep it calm and structured with no surprises.

Speaking *their* language will make them comfortable and more likely to work with you rather than against you.

Values Iceberg – What we value in life drives our beliefs which drive our actions.

Sidney Simon said (not to be confused with '*Simple* Simon said'!):

'*Ultimately it is our values that give us the stars by which we navigate ourselves through life.*'

Here's a list of ideas that might help you understand just how important it is to know what you truly value in your life.

- Values govern ALL human behaviour. They provide the **drive** that motivates us to take action. Values also provide our evaluation criteria after we have taken action.

- We are continually **communicating** and behaving in different ways towards ourselves and others. If these ways of communicating and behaving do not match our values or the values of others, then there is likely to be some form of conflict.

- All **emotion** is triggered by events that either align or clash with our values. E.g. If we value safety we get angry when someone puts us at risk. If we value order we are happy when our kids tidy up after themselves. If we value love then we are sad when someone we love rejects or leaves us.

- Values are the way we **differentiate** good and bad, appropriate and inappropriate. They are those things we live up to. They are the ideas in which we are willing to invest time, energy and resources so we can realise them.

- Our values are the mental **checklists** we have for choosing role models, or companies to purchase goods from, or friends to socialize with.
- Values are our attractions or repulsions in life, about what is **important** and what is not.

- Values can change depending on the **circumstances**. You probably have certain values about what you want in a relationship and what you want in business, and they are often not the same. For example, I might value structure and predictability in my business, but flexibility and unpredictability in my relationships.

- The way you **prioritise** your values can change with age and experience. When I was ten I valued my bike, at sixteen my girlfriend was at the top of the list and at 35 it was my family.

The values test:

❖ **How do you demonstrate your values in your life?**

In other words, if someone was watching you from a distance, what would they see you doing that would indicate to them that you held a particular value? For example, if you held the value of *Health*, would they see you, say... going to the gym three times a week, or... eating healthy food. And what about if *Love* was one of your values? Would they see you telling people that you loved them, or... doing things for those you love?

❖ **How do you feel when you don't demonstrate them?**

Now that you have identified some behaviours that indicate that you demonstrate your values in your life; how do you feel when you realise that you are not doing these things? To continue the *Health* example, how would you feel if you didn't go to the gym at all when you had promised yourself that you would? ...or you started smoking. And if you really value *Love*, but find yourself being unloving to someone you really care about, how does that make you feel?

❖ **How do you feel when you do demonstrate them?**

And again, based on demonstrating your values, how do you feel when you do the things that indicate that you are aligning with them? When you do go to the gym and do the things that will keep you healthy and you do act and speak lovingly toward people you care about, is that an uplifting experience?

The more we do things that align with and demonstrate our values, the better we feel about ourselves and our lives. Be accepting of others and their behaviours as you will probably find that they are attempting to live according to their own values. When they don't align with their own values, or yours, be aware that as a consequence, they probably go through the same mental struggle as we all do. And as I said back in Behavioural Blends, we didn't have much control on how our basic view of the world developed; and even our ability to modify our behaviour was shaped way back between conception and puberty.

Now list your Top Ten Values

1.
2.
3.
4.
5.
6.
7.
8.
9.
10.

And now return to page 107 and do the Values Test on the above list of your own Top Ten Personal Values.

So... how do you use your Values to improve your life?

1. To live a happier, healthier and more fulfilling life:

- Identify your top ten values

- Consciously demonstrate these values in all your actions

2. To enjoy happier, healthier and more fulfilling relationships:

- Identify the core values of those around you (If you're not sure, you could ask them!)

- Ensure your actions match their values

Pause Button

 The Pause Button is a deceptively simple yet amazingly powerful technique for assisting you to remain calm and focussed no matter what is going on around you.

There are at least two different types of Pause Button:

1. You can push an imaginary button that makes you:

Stop – breathe – focus (on facts) – remain calm

Use it whenever you need to engage the brain before putting mouth or body into gear.

2. You can push a physical Pause Button that changes the way you feel and it helps you to cope differently with a stressful or challenging situation.

Here's how you can create your own Pause Button:

The main principle is that, before you can engage in effective communication with another person, particularly in a stressful situation, you need to be calm and centred in yourself. Applying a Pause Button to your life will allow you to stand in the eye of the storm and remain focussed and alert, just like I had to when the storm hit me on the mountain.

How can you use this in everyday life?
What would it be like if you could create pictures in your mind that make you feel the things you want to feel any time you want to feel them? What we're going to talk about next is actually a continuation of something we learned earlier from the Lemon Man. It's a little trick that most of the greatest sports people, actors and presenters in the world use when they want to feel at their best just before, and during, an event they want to perform well in. They pay thousands of pounds to learn how to do this, and BJ, you're going to get it FREE with this session!

You can either memorise these next few paragraphs and then do it, or you can ask someone else to read it to you. Let's try it now.

Make yourself comfortable in your chair, take a deep breath, and gently close your eyes. I know it might feel a bit strange to be sitting there with your eyes closed, but just put that out of your mind and see whatever you are picturing fading away into blackness.

Now... I want you to remember a time when you felt really calm and happy; a time when everything seemed to be going well. Mentally return to that moment as if you are re-living it, right now. See who is there, what is happening, what is around you and what can you hear? Create a little five second video of the time that these good feelings are at their strongest... and now replay it several times, each time feeling all the great feelings that you were experiencing at the time.

Now I want you to play this video again, but this time in slow motion. When you get to the part where the feelings are strongest I want you to imagine that you are holding that feeling between your thumb and forefinger. Hold it tight for a couple of seconds... and now release it. Keep repeating this process four or five times at least, each time really feeling the emotions. Enjoy these good feelings for a couple of seconds... and now gently bring your awareness back to what's going on around you and start opening your eyes.

That's it. Simple huh? We have now 'anchored' that feeling into your sub-conscious. By squeezing your thumb and forefinger together again you should immediately see and feel the 'good feeling' video all over again. Do it once more, instantly, just for practice.

From now on, when something actually happens that could potentially upset you, I want you to squeeze your thumb and forefinger and instantly picture and feel your 'good feeling' video.

Practice

Here's something that really helped me to master this technique. Remember (or imagine) the worst thing you have been called or that has been said to you (or you could be called or could be said to you) by another person.

Imagine yourself in that scene again, begin to feel the things you felt as they started to say these things, and now… Push your Pause Button. It's impossible to feel bad if your mind is focussed on something good.

Remember, your whole life exists in your thoughts. What happens is not nearly as important as how you perceive or think about what happens and how you choose to feel about what happens.

So... how do you use your pause button?

Whenever you feel stressed or you are starting to panic you can:

1. Stop whatever you are doing, take a deep breathe. As you let it out, focus on all the muscles in your body and imagine your breathe is taking away all the tension and feel your muscles relaxing. Now say or do whatever it is you planned to say or do, but with a new sense of calm.

Or...

2. Imagine something that makes you feel good. Fully experience all the feelings that go with this picture or short video. Feel the 'feel good' chemicals running through your body as a result of picturing these images. There is no room for stress and panic chemicals if you are flooding your body with positive and uplifting chemicals.

Whadayawant?

Talk about what you want, not what you don't want. How often do we hear people talk about what they don't want instead of

what they want? So many times you will hear them discuss the problem far more than they discuss the solution. There are probably thousands of books, movies, television shows and training courses that extol the virtues of positive thinking, and yet so many of us still have trouble staying focussed on success and happiness instead of the opposite.

In Spanish festivals they often close the streets off with huge cage-like structures where you can safely watch the bulls running and the brave (and sometimes foolish) people who are being chased by them. They dash across the street with the bull in hot pursuit and dive between the bars just before it catches them. It seems that they only focus on the gap between the iron bars as they run at full throttle and then cleverly turn sideways to slip through to safety. It is much more effective for them to see what they want – the gap – than see what they don't want – the hard iron bars. By the way, I'm not condoning or criticising the 'bull-running' practice, but it is a good example of focus by both participants!

Other examples of being careful of what we focus on:
Does a high jumper focus on sailing high over the bar, or running into the bar? Does a successful businessman focus on profit or avoiding bankruptcy? Does a racing driver focus on the road or the fence? Will we be better influencers if we focus on what people do well rather than what they don't do well?

So... Whadayawant and how do you get it?

Be careful what you picture in your mind. There is a part of your mind/body that doesn't understand fake or imagined and takes everything as real. Make sure what you picture is really what you want.

Note: It doesn't work to picture what you don't want and imagine it not happening. It's too late – your mind already has a picture of what you don't want and will probably start creating it for you.

To start with, listen. Become aware of the words and language you and others use and then translate them before you open your mouth to speak. Examples:

- ✓ When someone asks you how you are, you could say 'Well' or 'Great thanks' or 'Fantastic!' instead of saying 'Not bad.'
- ✓ When someone asks you what you want to eat, you could say: 'I feel like something sweet' rather than saying 'I don't want anything salty'.
- ✓ When someone asks what you are good at, tell them. Don't make a list of what you are not good at.
- ✓ When someone asks directions, tell them where to turn, not where not to turn
- ✓ Define the problem but discuss and focus on the solution.

Get the picture? The general rule is:

Talk about a picture of success.

What 4 Feedback – simple, structured and effective

What is Feedback?
This is a slightly longer segment than the others, mainly because it is one of the most important. Feedback comes under the heading of Communication. Feedback is the world's way of communicating with us and us with it. But first, let's clear up something. Feedback has had some bad press over the years, so let's start with what it is not.

Feedback is not: opinion / abuse / innuendo / assumptions / manipulation / sarcasm...
Feedback is: ...just INFORMATION! In the broadest sense, it is every signal that reaches our brain via our senses.

Here's what the Compact Oxford English Dictionary says about:
Feedback – 1. information given in response to a product, performance etc., used as a basis for improvement. **2.** the modification or control of a process or system by its results or effects.

So... if it is just information, and is 'a basis for improvement', how can it be good or bad? As Shakespeare said:
'There is nothing either good or bad but thinking makes it so.'

Here is *my* feedback about feedback: The way we use the word in our daily lives I believe generally means: *Factual information about an event or what someone said or did including the effect that it had. It is intended to reinforce or change behaviour.*

In the corporate world you will even hear it labeled Performance Feedback i.e. it is information about something that was done, *not* about the person. And if the information leads to improvement, then it must be good!

ALL feedback is about the behaviour of a person or a thing. My back aches when I sit too long. It gives me feedback about my behaviour that informs me that I should probably move (change my behaviour) to alleviate the pain. Black clouds give us feedback that a storm is coming. If someone has a bad attitude, how do I know? Their behaviour gives it away – the frown, the use of aggression or sarcasm, their body language – and it gives me a message that something is going on inside their head that makes them *feel* like they need to use that behaviour. Their, and our, behaviour is a window into the unseen world of our thoughts and feelings. We usually add the emotion unnecessarily to the giving or receiving of feedback. (Although, emotion itself is feedback – information that tells us how someone feels.) But, if we only see the information, how can it affect us? 'Sticks and stones...etc'

Just like a rocket sends feedback to the control room so it can be kept on course, so the world sends us feedback to keep us on course. You'll never hear a train crying because it doesn't like being told it's on the wrong track! And...

Even if you're on the right track,
you'll get run over if you just sit there!
-Will Rogers

Everyone agrees with TOM!

TOM gives us What 4!

What happened > What happened next > What now > What for

In all relationships feedback is a partnership process involving two or more people investing the same amount of energy – we need to build a trusting relationship with the other partner. Feedback and Trust are integral to the process of creating an atmosphere of co-operation to achieve the objective.

Feedback is about:

A) maintaining relationships (Trust)

B) producing results (Objectives) and...

C) providing a reason for producing the results (Motivation)

But note: Before you deliver any feedback you will need to build trust by really listening and then apply your *Pause Button* so that you come across as being calm, assertive and in control of your emotions.

Building Trust with Engaged Listening

Engaged listening is not only about listening to what someone else is saying. It's also about making it easy for someone to listen to you and remember what you are saying (your *feedback*). It doesn't make sense to open your mouth unless you have really listened. The adage is *'Two ears and one mouth – should be used in that proportion.'*

Listening is about focussing and engaging i.e. you need to *do it*, not just expect it to happen because you can *hear*. You need to let them know you are listening by what you say and how you react. Breaking their conversation up into a maximum of 3-4 chunks, each chunk with its own **key word,** will make it easy for *you* to understand and remember what *they* are saying.

And now that you are operating with your head full of useful and relevant information (because you have really listened), you can make intelligent comments. Break up your own message (or feedback) into a maximum of 3-4 chunks, each chunk with its own **key word.** This will make it easy for *them* to understand and remember what *you* say. And remember the three rules of getting your message across:

✓ *Tell 'em what you're gonna tell 'em (Key words)*

✓ *Tell 'em. (Chunks)*

✓ *Then tell em what you just told 'em (Key words again)*

Or, just like the newsreaders on TV:

Headlines, Details, Headlines again.

Engaged Listening looks a bit like this:

Focus

- Identify the 3-4 main chunks
- Pick out and memorise three or four key words to match those chunks

Reflect

- Make encouraging gestures and verbal responses
- Ask questions that require more than one word answers

Summarise

- Restate what they said in your own words
- Explain your understanding of what was said

Listen like an elephant…
…with big ears and
a good long memory!

119

And now you're ready to deliver your Feedback
Remember, this is a two-way process involving both parties. It is not about telling the other person how the world appears according to you. For it to work, both of you need to have successfully negotiated the listening stage, then, deliver your feedback using the:

What 4 Checklist

What happened – describes the behaviour that you want to talk about. Notice that this is about an aspect of their *behaviour*, not their personality or your opinion of them. If they haven't seen the relevance or the full repercussions of this original action, they might think, 'So what?' They really need to know the:

What happened next – This is what resulted from *What happened*. The implications, detail and explanation of the *What happened*.

What now – What behaviour needs to be changed or continued? Without this, how is anything going to change or how are they going to know which particular behaviour needs to change, or alternatively, is worth continuing?

What for – Why change or continue? What will be the benefits to them? This part is probably the most important, but is most often missing from feedback. Without a strong motivational factor – the WIIFM (What's In It For Me?) – why should they change? We only change or continue our behaviour if there is a strong *What for* – a compelling motivational factor that is important to ourselves, not to someone else. Sure, others may get something out of it too, but then we get the credit and to feel good because we instigated it. It is our reward.'

How does it look in practice?
Imagine someone who works for you, let's call him Ralph, and you have a problem with his punctuality. It might sound a bit like this:

'Hi Ralph thanks for coming in. Everything OK?'
Ralph mumbles that he is OK.
'Great. Well, there's something I want to discuss with you'
Tell him **What Happened** – 'Last week it seems that you were late to work on Tuesday, Thursday and Friday.'
Tell him **What happened next** – 'As you probably know, when you are late, it causes problems because no-one else can start until *you* have started. This means we don't squeeze as many lemons which causes a loss in revenue. A loss in revenue means that we won't be able to pay bonuses to you or your team.'
Discuss the **What Now** – 'So how are we going to fix this? If we find a solution quickly...'
Work out the **What for** – '...we can probably catch up what we lost last week and you and your team will still be able to get your monthly bonus.'

Of course Ralph would probably want to say something and there would be conversation based around these four stages, but if they are all there, your chances of communicating successfully are greatly enhanced.

Feedback and Behavioural Blends
It is also useful to think about the style of person you are giving feedback to. If you have a rough idea of their usual behaviour patterns, you will have some idea of the most effective way of giving them feedback and you can choose an appropriate influencing strategy or method of delivering feedback. e.g...

Everyone agrees with TOM!

If they have *Control* glasses on, speak *Control* language – concise and result focussed.

If they are seeing a *Perfect* world, give them accurate details in the correct manner.

If it's *Entertainers* glasses they are wearing, make it positive and suggest that others will appreciate their changes.

If they are in *Mediate* mode, give them structure, routine and a peaceful life.

And remember, we often wear at least two different pairs of these 'behavioural style' glasses at any one time giving us different blends at different times on different days in different situations.

Tip: To make sure you are communicating in the most effective language, look back at the Behavioural Styles (page 102), identify the types of things that this style is interested in, and focus your conversation on these things. And finally…

Getting feedback the way you want it
Of course, the people who give you feedback may not know this process, but you can also use the What 4 Feedback Model as a tool for getting feedback the way you want it. By adding a question mark to each of the four *Whats*, you can steer the giver into giving you the feedback in a structured manner. If they are dumping a whole lot of information on you that doesn't seem to make sense, then just slow them down by asking:

'So… *What happened* exactly? …then…'and *what happened next?'* or 'What did that cause to happen?'…which leads to: 'What can we do *now*? …and finally, 'What *for*? What do you see as the main benefits to me/us?'

So... How do you use What 4 Feedback?
What happened – describe the behaviour or situation

What happened next – describe what resulted from *What happened*

What now – discuss the behaviour that needs to be changed or continued

What for – give the reason to change or continue and identify the benefits to **them**!

VISTA

And now that you have reached your objective it is important to acknowledge the achievement of every step and the attainment of the final goal.

Visualised – Does success match the mental picture you started with? Does it look, sound, feel, smell and taste like you expected? In this imaginary scene, who is there, what is happening and most importantly – how does it feel emotionally?

Inspirational – This aspect is a result of the scene you originally visualised. Did you feel inspired along the way? Were you inspired into action at every stage?

Specific – What can you learn from the specific steps or stages you passed through to match your vision? Did all the smaller achievements combine to give you your all important 'feel good factor' and spur you on toward your major vision of success?

Time bound – Did the deadlines on each specific step, as well as the final outcome, keep you motivated? Were they just far enough out of reach to give you an eventual sense of accomplishment, but not so far as to de-motivate you?

Assessable – Each time you achieved a specific or time-bound step, did you acknowledge yourself and celebrate the moment? Did you notice your progress? Did that moment of celebration give you confidence, lift you and move you forward? And now that you have reached your final destination, how does it feel? Make sure you stop long enough to appreciate your success.

So… how do you use VISTA?
Here are some examples to illustrate how you can use the exact same process for absolutely *every* goal, objective or outcome you want to achieve. No exceptions. Expect and visualise success and it is yours.

You decide to go on a holiday on a tropical island.
V – Picture yourself laying on the beach - cocktail in your hand, sunscreen on, warm sun, blue sea, smile on your face, people there who you care about and who care about you.
I – Feel the excitement the vision generates. If it doesn't, change your vision.
S – Make a list of tasks: Book time off, ring travel agent, organise visa, buy ticket, book hotel, buy clothes… and start doing them.
T – Today, book time off and ring bank; tomorrow, visit travel agent; Wednesday, book flights and accommodation; Thursday, organise visa; July 30, pack; August 1, Go!
A – Is vision creating excitement and action? Check at each specific and time-bound point that a) it is done and b) you congratulate and reward yourself for ticking it off your list.

Everyone agrees with TOM!

> **Imagine you are reorganising the office procedures:**
>
> V – Picture what the office will look and feel like after you have made the changes. Imagine you are eavesdropping on a conversation about the amazingly effective new office systems. What are people saying? How good does it make you feel?
>
> I – Really feel what it is like to work in the new office and let that be the feeling you are trying to match by bringing the new procedures into operation.
>
> S – Work backwards from the vision and identify all the things that need to happen in order:' *I'll feel good when the staff feel good. For them to feel good one thing I could do is make sure the office machines function well. For them to function well I'll have to have them serviced. To have them serviced we'll have to set time aside. To know when and how much time to set aside I'll have to ring the service company. First I'll have to find out their number.'* Now reverse the order and compile an ordered list of every step along the way. Repeat this for every part of the vision; even the small parts.
>
> T – Place a time limit on each step, but make it realistic - enough that it stretches you but not too much that it is stressful and de-motivating.
>
> A – Congratulate yourself and anyone else involved as each milestone is reached no matter how small or insignificant you may feel it is.

You want to boost total profit in the sales department by 30% this year

V – Picture the meeting where the figures are announced. See the graph on the PowerPoint slide curving up sharply from the time you took over the project. Feel the bonus cheque in your hand and the smile on the boss's face as he hands it to you.

I – Feel the sense of satisfaction and pride as everything in your vision becomes real.

S – To experience all the above we will have to achieve 30% increase in profit. 30% increase equals £360 000. £360 000 over 12 months is £30 000/mth. Divided by 10 sales staff is £3000/mth each. At average profit/sale of £1000 this is 3 extra sales. At an average of 10 calls per sale this equals 30 calls which is an extra 7.5 calls per week which equals approximately 1.5 calls per person per day… It doesn't look so huge now does it?

T – Time-bind each step above e.g. Write agenda for sales meeting by Monday; distribute it Tuesday; meeting Friday; start making calls Monday week; review progress 30th of month; report successes to team and company 1st of month…

A – Celebrate everything! – even the calls that amount to nothing. It's a numbers game – the larger the numbers, the larger the size of your cheque!

You are 16 and you want to pass your high school exams.

V – Picture yourself opening the letter telling you that you have not only passed, but have received excellent grades. See the smiles on the faces of your friends and family as you tell them. Maybe even see what results from your good grades e.g. getting a scholarship or your parents buying you an expensive gift as a reward for all your hard work.

I – Feel the sense of pride and achievement and especially feel the excitement the vision generates. If it doesn't, change your vision. Make sure it inspires you into action (study).

S – Make a list of tasks you will need to do to achieve your vision; find a coach for your weaker subjects and book time with them; Read books and articles on how to learn and remember faster; Hang out with other people who want to succeed and are prepared to put in the work required.

T – Set coaching times and study periods into your diary/timetable. (yes, it is a good idea!) Divide your study time into stages and put a deadline for each point on your *Specific* list e.g. By then I will have studied and will understand X and by then I will have studied Y etc.

A – Assess to ensure that the vision is still creating inspiration, excitement and action? Check at each specific and time-bound point that a) it is done and b) you congratulate and reward yourself for ticking it off your list. e.g. If you ask someone to test you and you do really well, give yourself a short break, go see a friend or buy yourself something you like – anything that makes you feel rewarded for effort. It will encourage you to put in even more effort when you can see the results of your actions.

7

BJ's New Day

TOM and BJ got together for a couple of hours every month to check on BJ's progress and to discuss new challenges. TOM was also on hand to offer congratulations when things were going well and encouragement when it seemed like they weren't. They are meeting again at the end of BJ's six-month contract with TOM.

'Remembering and using all the models was relatively easy,' begins BJ, 'but the real test came when I used them at work, at home and on the golf course.' And just as TOM had started his first coaching session with BJ, he again poses him the same question.

'So… what does a typical day look like for you now? How did all your agreements go after you applied everything you have learned?'

Here's what BJ said…

1. Agreement with self to get up on time linked to agreement with company to be at work on time.
I know I'm a heavy sleeper, so I decided to be like MAL and took response-ability. I bought an alarm clock with big bells on it and I have to get out of bed to go over to the dressing table and turn it off. I also bought a spare battery to put in if

the warning light comes on. And just in case it doesn't go off, I have the alarm on my mobile phone set to go off five minutes after my alarm clock.

2. *Agreement with wife to get milk and bread on the way home.*
I know my wife is a bit more detail conscious than I am and she probably has her *Perfect* glasses on a lot of the time. I often see things through *Entertain* glasses, but I know that if I take more response-ability for remembering and I write messages down, it works! (And it keeps my wife happy too!). Instead of using words though, I draw a quick sketch of a cow sitting on a toaster and I stick it in the lid of my briefcase so it will remind me to buy milk and bread.

3. *Agree with kids to take them to the pool.*
I'm becoming more confident at getting things done and I guess I trust myself a little more. I think my kids are starting to trust me again too because they have started asking me to pick them up again from the pool. Sometimes I have to ring them and adapt the plan, but I always remember to keep the agreement. It's better because we all know what's going on and we get to spend more time together now I'm more organised and reliable.

4. *Agreement to pick up friend and drive him to the station.*
MAL trusts me a bit more now and always waits for me because he knows if I am late, there is a genuine problem. I've started taking more pride in my appearance and looking like someone who can be trusted. I don't commit to things I won't be able to do, so that means I am more effective at the things I agree to do. And, because I know what it's like to be unreliable, I have more empathy and accept that people

really are doing their best with what they know, and I haven't got it perfect yet either.

5. *Agreement with rail company to be polite to rail staff.*
I've started renewing my rail ticket at night when I get off the train and there's no queue. This means, even if I get held up in traffic, I'm rarely late. And even the traffic doesn't annoy me any more. I live in a country with about as many cars as people, so of course there is going to be traffic. (What was I expecting?) This means that even if I am caught up with other people who are angry, or if a situation arises where once I would have become irritated, I press my Pause Button, remain calm and use the What 4 feedback structure to communicate my point of view. Consequently I have no problems with the rail staff and no problem with my...

6. *Agreement with rail company to buy ticket before boarding train.*
Not late, have ticket, not rushing, no problem. I trust myself now to be on time, I know what I have to do to stay out of trouble with the law and my motivation is that I won't have to pay another stupid fine!

7. *Agreement with boss to complete a major project.*
Because I have regular planning meetings with my boss now, we always have the same picture of where we are going and what the end result will look like. This mutual vision inspires us and makes it feel like we are actually on the same side. From that position it is easier to get the specifics nailed down and set deadlines for each stage so we can assess our progress. By the time we reach our goal we feel like we have truly earned our rewards. I also realise that it's my responsibility to make this project happen, not my boss or

my team, so I've stopped blaming others and justifying poor results. A friend of mine once said. 'The best way to deal with responsibilities is to understand that you have responsibilities – that's part of living.'

8.   Agreement with colleague to complete a document for her.
I've always known that Mary was different to me, but up until our sessions I never really understood exactly how she was different. Understanding that she wears her Mediate glasses a lot of the time has really helped. I don't mind a bit of chaos around me – it's sort of exciting in a way. But Mary is a bit quieter than me and likes order and keeping things running smoothly. By trying to think like she does I can understand what winds her up and avoid it. This way the team runs smoother and everyone stays happy and definitely more productive. I completed the document the way she wanted, not the way I wanted. No problem.

9.   Agreement with team to email them with the report from the monthly managers' meeting before their own team meeting later today.
By doing the things I have promised to do (I got the report to them) and not promising what I can't deliver, my team has more trust and respect for me. I get the monthly report to them now because I know how much it means to them, but for each of them it satisfies a different set of Values. It just so happens that the four people in my team each have a tendency to lean towards different styles. The one that leans toward Control wants to know if he's been *successful* and how much the bonus is. The one leaning towards Perfect wants to know if she is doing things *right*. The one with a mainly Entertain perspective wants to know if he is *liked* and if there are any exciting projects coming up. And the

Mediator perspective wants to make sure that the whole *team* is doing well. Keeping them all happy means that I now have a well functioning team.

10. Agreement with cusTOMer to buy a batch of old stock.

My cusTOMer bought all the old stock this month. It is simple really – TOM does the selling. When I build enough trust with the cusTOMer, set WIIFU objectives that work for both of us and find the cusTOMer's motivation (benefits to them) for buying, job done!

I noticed that this cusTOMer tends to have a Feeling Focussed world-view – Entertain and Mediate – so I showed her how this product would look good for her team and that she would get the credit for the thinking of it. It would also add some colour to her range of current offerings and brighten an otherwise drab display. She seems to trust me more now because I have her objectives in mind, I speak in her feeling focussed language and it's much easier to motivate her to buy when I know what she values. She really didn't want to know the specifications, only how it would make her cusTOMers feel. She bought the lot and will take next month's too!

11. Agreement with my team to present the objectives for the next three months.

Today I ran a Behaviourally Blended meeting. I painted a picture of success that appealed to everyone in the meeting. I gave only four main bullet points up front and told them the meeting would only take 10 minutes. This satisfied the one wearing Control glasses. I then quickly, concisely and efficiently added detail to the bullet points using slides that I had double-checked for inaccuracies before the meeting. This seemed to stop Mr Perfect glasses asking so many questions and fulfilled his need for information. I used an animated voice, coloured slides with images and laced my presentation with a bit of humour. This kept the Entertainer's glasses from fogging up. And because everyone else was happy, the woman with the Mediate glasses felt very relaxed and came up with some great ideas. Every meeting should be this quick and productive!

12. *Agreement with old lady to give me the right directions.*
I had to stop and get directions one night on the way to a meeting. I asked this old lady who was waffling on and kept changing her mind. I decided to use a variation of the What 4 model – in reverse. I asked her if she knew the fastest way to the hall. (the What for / the 'Why I should go this way?') And then I said 'Which way do I go now?' (What now?) Then 'Which way do I turn?' (What next?) and 'What will the last turn be?' (What then?) By asking clear direct questions of what I needed to do, I didn't give her an opportunity to talk about what not to do. I memorised the four steps of the directions and got there in plenty of time.

13. *Agreement with police to drive my car in a way that abides by the traffic laws.*
Well, because I am running early I can concentrate on what I'm doing and remember that the speed limit has changed along this stretch of road. I drive past a whole bunch of cars that have been pulled over for speeding. I don't laugh though – that was me six months ago. I'm learning to accept that we all need to learn something. We just get our lessons at different times and in different ways.

14. Agreement with wife to be home on time.
After my meeting I pick up the kids from the pool and head home. It feels good when I do what I say I'm going to do. I'm starting to get a reputation as a reliable dad. It's interesting that even little successes make me feel better. I've heard that Stress and Success can't really exist happily together. If I succeed in losing weight then I don't need to be stressed about my weight. If I'm successful at getting paid the money I want then I don't need to be stressed about not having any money. Kept agreements lead to more kept agreements.

15. Agreement with Department of Internal Revenue to pay taxes.
I think I'm finally starting to get it – it really is a cause and effect universe. If I want the positive logical consequence of doing something (the reward) I will probably have to do something to get it. Even winning the lottery involves buying a ticket. And equally, if I don't want the negative logical consequences of doing (or not doing) something... I've had more time to get things done recently because I get the first lot of things done that gives me time to get the second lot of things done. It really is just like a long chain reaction.

Sure, some things in life are just dumped on me I guess, but then I can do something as well – I can choose to respond instead of react. I can choose to do something to change it or not. Either way, there is always a choice. And of course the ultimate choice is a choice of attitude. I can complain and blame and justify as much as I like, or... I can choose to chalk it up as another life lesson. While I'm here there are going to be lessons – one after another. Some lessons I will like and some I won't, but there will always be something to learn. The sooner I realise that and accept that that's the way it is, the more enjoyable and productive my life will become. I'm choosing to be more like MAL and less like the old BJ. Maybe I should change my name! Anyway, there are no nasty letters from the taxation department this time, so I don't choose to lose my temper or throw anything, so I don't break any vases! But... I jam my fingers in the door, and where once I would probably have gone off my head and kicked the door (and then hurt my foot) I now take a deep breath, press my Pause Button, realise that it is my own silly fault... and I pour myself a cool drink.

16. Agreement with self and others to reward successes.
So I congratulate myself for having the sense to stay calm when I hurt my fingers – that makes me feel better. And because I'm not stressed about being late and angry because I have a tax bill, I now see things that make me feel good instead of bad. But one of the most important things I'm learning is to take the time to stop, acknowledge my successes and reap whatever reward I have set for reaching one of my assessable objectives. And I've started doing it with my team too, acknowledging their successes and encouraging them to appreciate their wins. I've worked out that my job as a manager is to find ways of providing them with the opportunity to succeed. My role is to make it easier to get the job done, not just tell them what to do.

17. Agreement with myself that I will lower my golf handicap and learn to play the piano.
It's quite amazing the correlation between practice and success. i.e. as soon as I start doing some, I start having some! My golf handicap has gone down, I can now play whole pieces on the piano without having to stop and apologise, and my self belief has gone up to match my

results. And do you know what keeps me going? The vision. In my mind I have this clear picture of myself standing on the stage and receiving my winner's trophy at the annual golf club dinner. And then the weirdest thing happens – the band invites me on stage to play the piano with them! Well, it might be a long way off yet, but the vision inspires me to keep at it.

18. Agreement with kids to communicate with them in a reasonable manner.

I've been using the What 4 model quite successfully for a while now at work, and now I'm using it at home too. I think in the past I have wanted people to do things just because I thought it was a good idea. But since I've been structuring my feedback more and making sure there's a strong *What for* to boost their motivation, I've been having a lot more success getting people to work with me.

So at home... I hit my Pause Button, sit down calmly with the kids and say, 'When you leave your room untidy, either Mummy or I have to tidy it. And if we have to spend time tidying, there probably won't be enough time to read you a story before bed. So, it's your choice (we are never too young to learn the power of choice). You can tidy your room and get a story or you can choose not to tidy your room and miss out on your story. Now if the room is kept tidy every night this week, we'll have time to go to the beach at the weekend. What do you think?' It's amazing. No arguments, no fighting, just results. The trick is to find a logical consequence (motivating factor) that works for them.

19. Agreement with self to pass my business school exams.

I'm finding that by using all ten intelligences I can actually learn much faster, remember more and I really enjoy it. And because I'm enjoying it, I want to go to the classes and I learn more... and then I enjoy it. It has all changed so much. I'm also finding that I don't have to study as much because I remember it all more effectively in the first place. Before I was treating it like school because that's what it reminded me of. It seemed back then that someone else was in charge of my learning and all I was required to do was turn up. Now I'm in control. It's my responsibility to learn, and I love it. I record the football match so I can watch it later.

20. Agreement with self to go to bed early so I can wake up easier in the morning.

Because of my new attitude to my day I seem to get so much more done. But it's funny, instead of being tired from the extra things I do, I seem to have more energy rather than less. I tend to choose what I do at night rather than just fall into the same pattern. I do still sometimes fall asleep in front of the television, but it's usually thinking about what a great day I've had and replaying all the things that worked, not the ones that didn't work. I'm also thinking about how great the next day is going to be and because my mind and body think it is really happening, I feel fantastic!

And you know, on top of all that, I really learned to be grateful and appreciative of what I *do have* and the things I *can do*, and especially about the progress I am making. My life really does exist in my thoughts, and as my brain doesn't know the difference between real and fake, I just get it to continually focus on success, whatever that looks like, in any task or relationship. My actions have no choice but to follow those thoughts.

BJ thanks TOM for all his coaching and support, but TOM is quick to point out that it is BJ who did all the work. Sometimes we are too quick to deflect the positive feedback we receive and attribute it to someone else. Yes, it is appropriate and noble to share the emotional rewards with others who have assisted us on our journey, but always be sure to congratulate the main player in this fanciful, long-playing drama called your life.

Everyone agrees with TOM!

So... What does it all mean?

Yes, I know that BJ's New Day looks all very idyllic and just about perfect, but isn't that what we are searching for – the elusive *perfect life*? When problems turn up we moan and complain as if believing that problems shouldn't occur. But in our lives there will always be problems, won't there? So problems are normal and therefore perfect and it follows that the perfect life is a life of problem solving. We seem to expect that everything should go our way. Why should it? It's great, in fact it's almost imperative, to live day to day always expecting things to go our way, but we can hardly be surprised when they don't. As Bill Gates once said in a speech to high school students,

'Life isn't fair. Get used to it!' What he didn't go on to say was,

'It isn't unfair either. It's just the way it is!'

TOM seems to have it right. He believes that the events of his life will match his expectations but is not surprised or upset when they don't. And when he sits back and evaluates what's happened, what's happening and what's going to happen, he revisits his toolkit looking for the perfect model or lesson to adapt his plan.

TOM, Patsy's Trusty PEA's, the distant VISTA objective, WIIFU, the LEMON man, MAL & BJ, the Triple 'A' bridge, the

Everyone agrees with TOM!

Behavioural Blender, the Values Iceberg, the Pause Button, the Whadayawant girl, the What 4 feedback ladder and the final VISTA, all have something to teach us. Keeping them in mind will assist us day to day – in the workplace or at home, in achievements or relationships – as we work towards 'having a good life' as we often refer to it.

And from the first page of this book:

When you get right down to it, isn't that what we mean when we say we're having a good life – we're getting things done and having a good time?

So… to you from me and TOM…

Index to Key Models

Everyone agrees with TOM!

Bibliography

(1) Page, R, 2002, The Enlightened Response, Chichester, UK

(2) Robertson, I, 2002, The Minds Eye, London, UK

(3) Shore, R. (1997). Rethinking the Brain: New Insights into Early Development. New York, NY: Families and Work Institute,

(4) Agarwal, I, MD American Academy Pediatrics, Early Brain and Child Development, Source: Article published on Internet

About the author

Ross Page has been examining what he calls the Life Creation Process, from various different perspectives, for most of his life. For much of the last twenty years he has worked with hundreds of companies and thousands of individuals all over the world, creating, fine-tuning, but most of all applying the techniques and principles that form the core of this book.

Delegates from many different countries and in various locations have experienced Ross' workshops and presentations. He currently lives in the United Kingdom and Spain and works internationally facilitating events focussed on a variety of topics including:

Leadership
Management
Personal Development
Communication
Team Building
CusTOMer Service

...or in fact any situation that requires the achievement of a practical result combined with the maintenance of healthy relationships.

This book is a culmination of living, loving, learning, thinking, writing and working to assist himself and others to 'get things done and have a good time'. Now he says, 'All we have to do is remember to keep applying it!'

Everyone agrees with TOM!

Who has benefited from the TOM Models?

Ross has worked with participants from numerous corporate and private organisations and groups, including:

Camp Eden Health Resort	Axa Finance
Tesco	Clear Mountain Health Lodge
Axa PPP Health Care	T-Mobile
Arriva Passenger Services	HM Treasury
Ericsson	First Direct Bank
KPMG	Rank Gaming
TNT Express	Allianz Cornhill Insurance
LloydsTSB	P&O Resorts
Zurich Insurance	General Motors
Royal College of Physicians	Axa Insurance
East Sussex County Council	Boden Clothing
Rolls Royce	Selfridges
Adams Childrenswear	UK Probation Service
Phillips	Institute Sales and Marketing
Nestlé	Generic Pharmaceuticals
Dunnhumby	The Sytner Group
Coors Brewing	Kew Gardens
London Tourism Network	Sandwell MBC
Methvens Bookstores (UK)	Goodey's Bookstores (NZ)
Westpac Bank (Aus)	Australia Post
Royal Bank of Scotland	Astra Zeneca
Kraft Foods	Institute Grocery Distributors
EMAP Radio	Matalan
Herbert Smith	Stead and Simpson
East Sussex County Council	Wealden District Council
The Co-op Group	Breeze & Wyles ...and more.

Email info@TOM.gb.com or visit www.TOM.gb.com

ISBN 1425121993-3